The Poets' Christ

DAVID WINTER graduated from King's College, London, before becoming an English teacher and eventually Head of Religious Broadcasting at the BBC. He is a regular contributor to Radio 4's 'Thought for the Day' and *The Church Times* 'Diary' as well as a variety of other broadcasts and publications. Now a priest in the Church of England and Honorary Canon of Christ Church Cathedral, Oxford, he has three children and two grandchildren. He and his wife Christine live in Oxfordshire.

The Poets' Christ

An anthology of poetry about Jesus

Compiled by David Winter

A LION BOOK

Published by
Lion Publishing plc
Sandy Lane West, Oxford, England
ISBN 0 7459 4284 9

First edition 1998 published
under the title *The Master Haunter*
This paperback edition 2000
10 9 8 7 6 5 4 3 2 1 0

Acknowledgments
Illustrations: Sarah Young

A catalogue record for this book is available
from the British Library

Typeset in Garamond ITC
Printed and bound in Great Britain by
Omnia Books Limited, Glasgow

Contents

Introduction

Jesus of Nazareth is one of the formative figures in the history of the human race – perhaps the *most* formative of all. Although his public activity lasted barely three years, and he left no writings of his own, his words – recorded by his followers – have profoundly influenced the world's thinking ever since. Leaving behind him only a handful of dispirited disciples, he appeared to be, by human standards, something of a failure. Yet within a single lifetime his message had been carried far across the ancient world, his followers could be found in every stratum of society in the Roman empire, and a movement had been born which, within a couple of centuries, would turn that world upside down.

Since that time the Church founded by his followers – and based not just on his teaching but on the impact of his death by crucifixion and their belief in his resurrection from death – has become beyond argument the most powerful religion in human history. As mankind enters the third millennium of the Christian era – even the calendar being set by the supposed date of the birth of Jesus – Christianity is by far the largest world religion, and is still growing.

Yet such triumphalist language contrasts sharply with the picture of Jesus evoked by the poets whose work forms this anthology. For many of them, in the words of Peter Porter, Jesus is the 'Master Haunter', the elusive, energizing, creative, suffering icon of humanity. Jesus called himself 'the Son of Man', the representative human being, the 'Proper Man', in Luther's strange phrase. That is the figure who haunts their imaginations – a man (and for many of them, of course, much more than just a man) who offers a key to the meaning of our existence, that elusive clue to the perennial search of the artist for connection, purpose and inner truth.

It has been a fascinating exercise to travel again through the rich fields of poetry in English in search of the 'Poets' Christ'. True to their calling, and as we might expect, there is no unanimity of vision, no consensus of truth, to be found in their work. Some are devout believers, celebrating and affirming the truths of a faith that shapes and informs their lives. Some are sceptical, though fascinated by the personality of Jesus and the imagery of his life and death. Some are openly hostile, at any rate to the Jesus offered by traditional Christianity and the Church. All find their places in this collection, often awkwardly alongside each other, because each in his or her own way is responding to the influence of Jesus. Some, in other words, are poems of faith; some are poems of exploration, and some are poems of honest doubt. As a convinced Christian myself, I felt excited and moved by all of them. Indeed, I suppose that is the crucial touchstone of my selection. There is no poem in this book which left me unmoved.

An Anthology about Jesus

I have described this as an anthology of poetry about Jesus. Just to say that is to invite any number of questions, some of which I have already begun to answer. What is poetry? How does one define it? How were the poems selected? What does it mean to say that it is 'about' Jesus? Is this another book of devotional verse, offering suitable material for framing on bedroom walls? Does it exclude poetry which is about Jesus but raises questions or doubts about him, rather than strengthening faith?

Simply to ask the questions is to begin to define the book. For this is an anthology of poetry, first and foremost. A fundamental criterion for inclusion has been that a piece of writing should be genuinely and recognizably poetry. Most of the poems in this collection are by recognized poets, those whose work has been published as poetry. Indeed, many of them are written by the acknowledged masters of English literature, ancient and modern. Some are by less well-known poets, of course, and one or two are by writers who, while not usually placed in the ranks of the poets, on this occasion (in my view) earned inclusion for a piece of genuine poetry.

What is Poetry?

Of course, that raises the eternal question: What is poetry? As a former teacher of English literature I have often wrestled with this dilemma. Some in the past would have defined poetry by form: does it rhyme, does it have a rhythm or metre? But clearly that will not do. Some writing that undoubtedly has the form of poetry (it rhymes, it has metre) is obviously not poetry – nursery rhymes, for instance, or couplets written in autograph albums. Equally, some writing which does not have either rhyme or metre is undoubtedly poetry: the psalms of the Hebrew scriptures, for instance, where the form is in the balance of image and idea rather than the sound of words: 'The heavens declare the glory of God / And the firmament proclaims his handiwork'.

Yet most of us can recognize poetry when we see or hear it, though that recognition can itself be a highly individual and personal thing. For me (and one can never go much beyond that), poetry is the distillation of ideas and connections in intensive language. Wordsworth called it emotion recollected in tranquillity, but that doesn't go far enough. Much poetry is far from tranquil, though emotion, in the sense of strong feeling, is clearly an indispensable element. But it is the way the emotion is handled that turns prose or verse into poetry. There is an economy, a distillation, an intensity about poetry that is utterly distinctive. The poet can say in a few words what you and I would struggle to express in hundreds. For me, the appeal of much modern poetry lies in that economy and intensity, which (to be honest) I often seek in vain in the work of such great poets as Milton or Pope.

I have tried to apply these criteria to the works included in this anthology. They are pieces of writing which connect ideas and images in powerful and intense language, throwing light on complicated or even obscure facets of truth. The poet is the great illuminator of human thought. In Blake's memorable phrase, poets see 'through the eye', not just with it.

For the purpose of this anthology I have excluded verse written primarily to be sung. Some hymns, especially those by such masters of the craft as Charles Wesley, Isaac Watts and John Mason Neale, are undoubtedly poetry: but the line had to be drawn somewhere. I have also excluded, on the whole, verse which, while greatly loved and cherished by Christians because of its message, falls short of the strict definition of poetry. I am thinking here of the often moving verses of a man like G. Studdert-Kennedy. There are always, of course, borderline decisions, and once or twice I have included work which seemed to me to demand inclusion for the force or perception of its insight rather than for pure poetic quality.

Poems about Jesus

Although all the poems in this collection are about Jesus, I have deliberately interpreted that criterion broadly. Some are descriptive, some devotional, some meditative, some interpretative, some sceptical… and some use images and ideas which spring directly from the life or teaching of Jesus, but employ them in a daring – and even shocking – way to the human condition. In other words, while some of these poems will offer comfort to the disturbed, others will disturb the comfortable. Poets, as a breed, are a questioning, tentative, awkward tribe. One has only to read the poems of Henry Vaughan or John Donne – devout Christians, beyond dispute – to see how tense and febrile a thing faith can be to the poetic soul.

In an anthology of poetry about Jesus it would be reasonable to assume that most of the authors would be Christians. And that is certainly so. Until the late eighteenth century, at least, there was little poetry written about Jesus that was not, in one way or another, intended to strengthen, interpret or celebrate faith. But it has been fascinating to see how, over the past two centuries, poets who were not conventionally Christian, or indeed were agnostics or even atheists, have returned again and again to ideas and imagery which arise from the story of Jesus. The 'pale Galilean', in Swinburne's evocative phrase, still has the power to earth the divine. We may speak of a post-Christian culture, but it has not yet found another image for its deepest longings and hopes.

It has been interesting to observe how, over the centuries, poets have concerned themselves with different aspects of that story. For the early English poets it was the birth of Jesus (and especially the role of Mary) and the suffering of the crucifixion, that absorbed their interest. For the poets of the sixteenth and seventeenth centuries it was largely issues of love, mercy and forgiveness. In the eighteenth century, it was the divine plan that fascinated. In the Victorian era there is surprisingly little in its greatest poets that is specifically about Jesus, though a great deal about God, duty, faith… and creation, not surprisingly in the age of Darwin. When we come to the poets of what might loosely be termed the modern era, we find a fresh interest in Jesus as teacher, healer, radical reformer and model of freedom and hope. This is especially true for poets from Africa and the Caribbean, though British, American and Australasian poets have also explored those themes. And to complete the historic circle, there is much use of the cross as a symbol of sacrifice, suffering and self-giving. For the modern poet, there is no cheap grace, no easy revolution, no real hope that has not been forged in the fire of suffering. All this says, of course, is that the poet is a child of the age, whether that age is the mystical Christian culture of the medieval world, or the swirling uncertainties of the age of technology and science.

English Poetry

This is an anthology of English poetry, which means that all of the poems were originally written in English. That includes the Old

English of the Anglo-Saxon period and the Middle English of Langland and Chaucer. This raises a problem for the anthologist: should the poems be printed as they were written, or translated into more accessible language? I have chosen the second option, while remaining aware that something is inevitably lost in the process. However, relatively few modern readers are able to understand the early forms of our present-day language. Rather than omit them completely, or print them in a form that few could enjoy, I have used versions which retain as far as possible the language and shape of the original, while enabling the modern reader to understand them. After all, the specialist scholar has access to the original texts, while the general reader may feel excluded from a wonderful and evocative field of poetry, which is part of the heritage of all English-speaking people. I have undertaken some of these translations myself, but also used some already published versions. These early flowerings of a truly English literature are too good to omit, both from a literary point of view, and for the quality of their insight into the spiritual significance of Jesus.

English poetry includes not only poetry from the earliest days of our language, but from all the places where it has taken root over the centuries. So this anthology includes a substantial amount of work by poets from America, Australia, New Zealand, South and West Africa and the Caribbean. The only qualification is that it should originally have been written in English. This also applies to poetry from Scottish and Welsh authors – in the case of Scots dialect poetry I have not presumed to attempt to anglicize it!

The Master Haunter

In editing this collection I have constantly had in mind a poem by a twentieth-century Australian-born writer, Peter Porter, because it encapsulates for me the purpose of the whole book. He calls his poem 'The Unlucky Christ'. It is a moving and perceptive exploration of the way in which many thinking people today approach the religious search. Porter understands his contemporaries:

> Some people can take straight off
> from everyday selfishness to
> the mystical, but the vague shape
> of the Professional Sorrower
> seems to interpose when I try
> such transport.

The world in which we live does not move easily into the mystical or spiritual realm, yet we, too, are spiritual beings and will never be completely human until we find meaning and purpose beyond ourselves. Porter senses, as do many of the modern poets, that Jesus Christ (the 'Professional Sorrower') may be the crucial – if for some unwelcome – key to that search:

I am... one... who has
come closer to him through suffering
and loathes the idea.

It is on this tentative, honest, troubled quest of the modern seeker that the poets can help us, for they feel more acutely, see more honestly, connect more imaginatively in that search than the rest of us. That does not mean that they are nearer to God, nor even nearer to the truth. But image, symbol and connection may help modern people where logic and reason fail. Indeed, it may be that, in the world of the new millennium, imagination will be a more effective guide to truth than reason. As Blaise Pascal wrote, 'It is the heart that perceives God, and not the reason.' In Martin Henry's words, we are left with an 'eerie universe' which is a projection of God's incomprehensibility. Yet we are still *capax Dei* – capable of encountering God. That is the ultimate human gift, and it is one which these poets, great and small, may help us to rediscover. And the one who is the subject of these poems, the Christ of history, faith and human experience, is, for many of them, an indispensable clue on the journey towards the truth.

Reading this Book

There are several ways to read an anthology. One can start by dipping in here and there, looking for a favourite poet or poem. Or one can start with the list of contents, choosing a period or theme as a point of entry. Or, of course (though more rarely, I suspect), the reader can start at the beginning and read it straight through. The compiler has no right to tell the reader how to approach what ought to be a supermarket of delights – with or without a shopping list, as it were, or as an enthusiastic browser, or as an 'impulse buyer'. It really doesn't matter very much.

As there are different approaches to reading a book like this, so there are also different categories of readers. Some will come to it primarily as poetry lovers, to explore the different ways in which the poetic imagination can choose to approach a subject like this. Some will come to it as convinced Christians, looking for light on the path of faith – or for the dark corners of doubt. Some will come to it because, while they are not conventional 'believers', they recognize that the history of the past 2,000 years has been deeply influenced, not to say shaped, by this elusive figure from Nazareth – and that the poets may help them to discover him in a way that sermons and scripture have so far not been able to.

I appreciate that some of the poems in this collection, especially by the modern poets, may at first reading seem quite incomprehensible to the reader not well versed in the tricks of the poetic trade. The solution is not to give up! At one level, poems aren't there to be 'understood' so much as absorbed, and (rather like learning a foreign language) one tends to find that constantly encountering the idiom is more important than mastering the grammar. In other words, re-reading a poem many times, until its ideas, images and sounds are familiar, will often yield a glimpse into the meaning that had at first proved elusive.

However readers come, and with whatever personal agenda, I hope they will find unexpected treasures in this collection. The criteria I have applied will probably mean that some omissions and inclusions are unexpected. There was never yet a poetry anthology that satisfied everybody. But I believe that these poems, spanning a thousand years of history and coming from every corner of the English-speaking world, will offer to the reader a unique approach to Jesus. What we are offered, in all its glorious diversity, is the haunting image of the 'Poets' Christ'.

Compiler's Note

The poems are arranged in sections according to their subjects, and within the sections in approximate date order, with the oldest poems first.

I am greatly indebted to many people who have suggested poems for this collection – too many to acknowledge individually. But I am especially grateful to Margaret Wallace, who allowed me to raid her splendid collection of religious verse. To her, and to all who made suggestions (whether or not they finally made it into the anthology), my warm thanks. You helped to make the task a thoroughly happy and rewarding one.

David Winter

o n e

The Birth

'The Secret Stair'

The 'facts' of the birth of Jesus are briefly told, if we are thinking of what is historically indisputable. He was born in the last year or two of the reign of Herod the Great (let's say, 4BC). His home town was Nazareth, in Galilee (hence his title 'Jesus of Nazareth'). The birth probably took place not in his own home but in Bethlehem, in Judea, some sixty miles away – one says 'probably' because, despite the clear gospel claim that Jesus was born in 'the city of David' (Bethlehem), and there is no real reason to dispute it, there is a lack of evidence for this from other sources. His mother was called Mary and his father was a carpenter, Joseph. After his birth we hear virtually nothing about him until he makes his appearance in the Jordan valley in AD27, and begins his brief but eventful 'public' life.

The Bible offers us two accounts of the circumstances of his birth, in the gospels of Luke and Matthew. They are very different in many details, though the place and the parents' names are identical. Luke's account offers Mary's perspective on the events, which is not surprising, as it is highly likely that he met her while they were both living in Ephesus, later in her life. Matthew's story centres on Joseph, and is concerned (some scholars would say obsessed) with possible parallels between the birth of Jesus and the prophecies of the Messiah in the Hebrew scriptures. The gospels of Mark and John are silent about the birth of Jesus, and it is only referred to obliquely in the rest of the New Testament. One does not get the impression that the early Church was very concerned about the details of the birth, though emphatic that Jesus was truly human ('born of a woman') and truly divine: 'In the beginning was the Word... and the Word was God... and the Word became flesh and dwelt among us.'

In the light of this, it may seem surprising that Christmas is such a major event in the Christian calendar, at any rate in the Western world. For many people in that culture, Christmas is the one occasion in the year when they would expect to be in church. And in the more traditional Catholic countries, the pervading image of Jesus is of the child Christ – *le petit enfant Jesu, el Nino*.

Most of the poetry about the birth of Jesus reflects these traditions, not surprisingly. In medieval times, when the cult of the Virgin was at its height, devotion to Mary was expressed most directly in her great role as the 'God-bearer' – 'Goddes mother', as our first poem describes her. This echoes the pictorial art of the time, of course. Mary, the iconic Mother, welcomed her children and introduced them to her Son. Jesus was either the babe in arms or – paradoxically – the final judge of all. In church after church he was either depicted as helpless in his Mother's arms, or sitting on a throne despatching sinners to the fires of hell. No wonder Mary was sought as a mediator between this awesome figure and his faltering followers.

The earliest poems in this section certainly reflect both this admiration for Mary and care for her priceless baby, upon whom the salvation of the world was to rest. But they also begin to tell the 'story' – perhaps we could say, The Story. Already they offer hints of what was in store: the suffering, death and agony that lay ahead for Jesus, and the heart-wrenching pain of the mother who was to stand by the cross and watch him die.

But they also set this birth against a wider backcloth: the concept of incarnation – God in human flesh. Some of these poets, like William Dunbar, simply celebrate it:

> And thank your Maker heartily;
> For he that ye might not come to
> To you is coming full humbly.

Or George Macdonald:

> O Son of man, to right my lot
> Naught but Thy presence can avail...

And how would that 'presence' come to us? In a haunting phrase Macdonald captures it beautifully: Jesus came down his 'own secret stair'. That 'stairway' was, of course, humanity, our flesh, the life of a true and real human being. That is the heart of the 'story' of Christmas, in Christian terms.

But it *is* essentially a story, as Carl Sandburg reminds us, and a story of 'thousands of years'. 'Why,' he asks, 'does the story never wear out?' Perhaps it takes a poet of this century, and of the new world, even to ask the question. His poem 'Star Silver' hints at its own answer – the story of Christmas makes connections that can speak even to a child: 'cross-lights of silver and green'. It touches us where we are most vulnerable, not just in the story of the birth, but in its incidentals – the barn and the feed-box, the 'mule's teeth on Bethlehem Christmas corn', the 'vagabond men of wisdom', and a 'baby there in swaddling clothes on hay'. Yes, it is sentimental, in one sense, but it is also fundamental. It touches human beings 'where they itch'. It speaks to the heart of human experience, sorrow and joy.

But it is more than simply a 'story', however warm and human that story might be. And it is more than that, much more, to many of the poets, especially the writers of more modern times as they struggle to grasp the meaning and the mystery of the incarnation and this strange narrative that encapsulates it. Three poems in this section illustrate the way in which the poet can 'fill out' that narrative with imagination and insight.

G.K. Chesterton's 'The House of Christmas' takes one small element of Matthew's story – the holy family's flight into Egypt to escape the wrath of Herod – to relate the divine experience of humanity to the fundamental human need for 'home':

> To the end of the way of the wandering star,
> To the things that cannot be and that are,
> To the place where God was homeless
> And all men are at home.

For Charles Causley, the words *'Christus natus est'* ('Christ is born') are written in bitter red on the 'squalling dark'. When we share the bread and wine of Communion we also share in some strange way the whole experience of humanity – his flesh is ours, our flesh is his:

> Silently we renew
> The ruined bread and wine;
> Take the huge-bellied child
> Whose flesh is yours, is mine.

W.H. Auden, in probably the most painful poem in this generally celebratory section, invites us to consider what this 'enfleshment' of deity meant for Jesus himself. Birth, after all, inevitably leads eventually to death – and this baby was destined, beyond anything else, to die. He puts these thoughts into the unlikely form of a lullaby, addressed by Mary to her new-born son:

> Dream. In human dreams earth ascends to Heaven
> Where no one need pray nor ever feel alone.
> In your first few hours of life here, O have you
> Chosen already what death must be your own?
> How soon will you start on the Sorrowful Way?
> Dream while you may.

I Sing of a Maiden

I sing of a maiden
 That is makeless:
King of all kinges
 To her son she ches.

He came all so stille
 There his mother was,
As dew in Aprìlle
 That falleth on the grass.

He came all so stille
 To his mother's bower,
As dew in Aprìlle
 That falleth on the flower.

He came all so stille
 There his mother lay,
As dew in Aprìlle
 That falleth on the spray.

Mother and maiden
 Was never none but she;
Well may such a lady
 Goddes mother be.

Anonymous (15th century)

Makeless: matchless
Ches: chose

The Virgin's Song

Jesu, sweete sone dear,
On poorful bed liest thou here,
    And that me grieveth sore;
For thy cradle is as a bere,
Ox and asse be thy fere:
    Weep I may therefòre.

Jesu, sweete, be not wroth,
Though I n'ave clout ne cloth
    Thee on for to fold,
Thee on to folde ne to wrap,
For I n'ave clout ne lap;
But lay thou thy feet to my pap
    And wite thee from the cold.

Anonymous (15th century)

On the Nativity of Christ

Rorate coeli desuper!
Heaven, distill your balmy showers!
For now is risen the bright day star,
From the rose Mary, flower of flowers;
The clear Sun, whom no cloud devours
Surmounting Phoebus in the East
Is coming from his heavenly towers:
Et nobis Puer natus est.

Archangels, angels and dominations,
Thrones, potentates and martyrs sere,
And all ye heavenly operations,
Star, planet, firmament and sphere,
Fire, earth, air and water clear,
To Him give loving, most and least,
That comes into so meek manner:
Et nobis Puer natus est.

Sinners be glad, and penance do,
And thank your Maker heartily;
For he that ye might not come to
To you is coming full humbly,
Your souls with His blood to buy
And loose you from the fiend's arrest –
And only of His own mercy:
Pro nobis Puer natus est.

William Dunbar (1465–1513)

From: A Hymn of the Nativity, Sung by the Shepherds

Welcome to our wond'ring sight
Eternity shut in a span!
Summer in Winter! Day in Night!
Heaven in Earth! and God in Man!
Great little one, whose glorious Birth,
Lifts Earth to Heaven, stoops heaven to earth.

Welcome, though not to Gold, nor Silk,
To more than *Caesar's* Birthright is.
Two sister-Seas of virgin's Milk,
With many a rarely-temper'd kiss,
That breathes at once both Maid and Mother,
Warms in the one, cools in the other.

She sings thy Tears asleep, and dips
Her kisses in thy weeping Eye,
She spreads the red leaves of thy Lips,
That in their Buds yet blushing lie.
She 'gainst those Mother Diamonds tries
The points of her young Eagle's eyes.

Welcome, (though not to those gay flies
Guilded i' th' Beams of Earthly Kings
Slippery souls in smiling Eyes)
But to poor shepherds, simple things,
That use no varnish, no oil'd Arts,
But lift clean hands full of clear hearts.

Yet when young *April's* husband showers
Shall bless the fruitful *Maia's* Bed,
We'll bring the first-born of her flowers,
To kiss thy feet, and crown thy head.
To Thee (Dread Lamb) whose Love must keep
The Shepherds, while they feed their sheep.

To thee meek Majesty, soft King
Of simple Graces, and sweet Loves,
Each of us his Lamb will bring,
Each his pair of silver Doves.
At last, in fire of thy fair Eyes,
We'll burn, our own best sacrifice.

Richard Crashaw (1612–49)

Carol

All this night shrill chanticler,
Day's proclaiming trumpeter,
Claps his wings and loudly cries:
'Mortals! mortals! wake and rise!
    See a wonder,
    Heaven is under;
From the earth is risse a sun
Shines all night, though day be done.

'Wake, O earth! wake, every thing!
Wake and hear the joy I bring;
Wake and joy, for all this night
Heaven and every twinkling light
    All amazing,
    Still stand gazing;
Angels, powers, and all that be,
Wake, and joy this sun to see.'

Hail, O sun! O blessed light
Sent into the world by night!
Let thy rays and heavenly powers
Shine in this dark soul of ours,
    For most duly
    Thou art truly
God and man, we do confess:
Hail, O Sun of Righteousness!

William Austin (1587–1634)

 *Ode on the Morning of Christ's Nativity*

The Shepherds on the Lawn,
Or ere the point of dawn,
    Sate simply chatting in a rustick row;
Full little thought they than,
That the mighty Pan
    Was kindly com to live with them below;
Perhaps their loves, or els their sheep,
Was all that did their silly thoughts so busie keep.

When such musick sweet
Their hearts and ears did greet,
    As never was by mortall finger strook,
Divinely-warbled voice
Answering the stringèd noise,
    As all their souls in blisfull rapture took.
The Air such pleasure loth to lose,
With thousand echo's still prolongs each heav'nly close.

Nature that heard such sound
Beneath the hollow round
    Of Cynthia's seat, the Airy region thrilling,
Now was almost won
To think her part was don,
    And that her raign had here its last fulfilling;
She knew such harmony alone
Could hold all Heav'n and Earth in happier union.

At last surrounds their sight
A Globe of circular light,
    That with long beams the shame-fac't night array'd,
The helmèd Cherubim
And sworded Seraphim,
    Are seen in glittering ranks with wings displaid,
Harping in loud and solemn quire,
With unexpressive notes to Heav'ns new-born Heir.

Such musick (as 'tis said)
Before was never made,
    But when of old the sons of morning sung,
While the Creator Great
His constellations set,
    And the well-ballanc't world on hinges hung,
And cast the dark foundations deep,
And bid the weltring waves their oozy channel keep.

Ring out ye Crystall sphears,
Once bless our human ears,
    (If ye have power to touch our senses so)
And let your silver chime
Move in melodious time;
    And let the Base of Heav'ns deep Organ blow
And with your ninefold harmony
Make up full consort to th'Angelike symphony.

John Milton (1608–74)

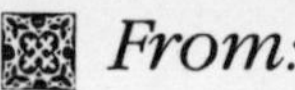

From: Messiah

A Sacred Eclogue in Imitation of Virgil's Pollio

Ye nymphs of Solyma! begin the song:
To heavenly themes sublimer strains belong.
The mossy fountains, and the sylvan shades,
The dreams of Pindus and Aonian maids,
Delight no more – O thou my voice inspire
Who touch'd Isaiah's hallowed lips with fire!
    Rapt into future times, the bard begun:
A Virgin shall conceive, a Virgin bear a Son!
From Jesse's root behold a Branch arise,
Whose sacred flower with fragrance fills the skies:
The ethereal spirit o'er its leaves shall move,
And on its top descends the mystic Dove.
Ye heavens! from high the dewy nectar pour,
And in oft silence shed the kindly shower!
The sick and weak the healing plant shall aid,
From storms a shelter, and from heat a shade.
All crimes shall cease, and ancient fraud shall fail;
Returning Justice lift aloft her scale;
Peace o'er the world her olive wand extend,
And white-robed Innocence from heaven descend.
Swift fly the years, and rise the expected morn!
Oh spring to light, auspicious Babe, be born!
See Nature hastes her earliest wreaths to bring,
With all the incense of the breathing spring:
See lofty Lebanon his head advance,
See nodding forests on the mountains dance:
See spicy clouds form lowly Saron rise,
And Carmel's flowery top perfumes the skies!
Hark! a glad voice the lonely desert cheers: –
'Prepare the way! a God, a God appears';
'A God, a God!' the vocal hills reply,
The rocks proclaim the approaching Deity.
Lo, earth receives him from the bending skies!
Sink down, ye mountains, and ye valleys, rise;
With heads declined, ye cedars, homage pay;
Be smooth, ye rocks; ye rapid floods, give way;
The Saviour comes! by ancient bards foretold!
Hear him, ye deaf, and all ye blind, behold!

Alexander Pope (1688–1744)

A Christmas Carol

Dark and dull night, fly hence away,
And give the honour to this Day,
That sees December turn'd to May.
If we may ask the reason, say,
The why, and wherefore all things here
Seem like the Spring-time of the year?

Why does the chilling Winter's morn
Smile, like a field beset with corn?
Or smell, like a Mead new-shorn,
Thus, on the sudden? Come and see
The cause, why things thus fragrant be:
'Tis He is born, whose quick'ning Birth
Gives life and lustre, public mirth,
To Heaven, and the under-Earth.

We see Him come, and know him ours,
Who, with His Sun-shine, and His showers,
Turns all the patient ground to flowers.

The Darling of the world is come
And fit it is we find a room
To welcome Him. The nobler part
Of all the house here, is the heart,
Which we will give Him; and bequeath
This Holly, and this Ivy Wreath,
To do Him honour; who's our King,
And Lord of all this Revelling.

Robert Herrick (1591–1674)

Rosa Mystica

'The Rose in a mystery' – where is it found?
Is it anything true? Does it grow upon ground?
It was made of earth's mould, but it went from men's eyes,
And its place is a secret, and shut in the skies,
In the Gardens of God, in the daylight divine
Find me a place by thee, Mother of mine.

But where was it formerly? Which is the spot
That was blest in it once, though now it is not?
It is Galilee's growth; it grew at God's will
And broke into bloom upon Nazareth Hill.
In the Gardens of God, in the daylight divine
I shall look on thy loveliness, Mother of mine.

What was its season, then? How long ago?
When was the summer that saw the Bud blow?
Two thousands of years are near upon past
Since its birth, and its bloom, and its breathing its last.
In the Gardens of God, in the daylight divine
I shall keep time with thee, Mother of mine.

Tell me the name now, tell me its name:
The heart guesses easily, is it the same?
Mary, the Virgin, well the heart knows,
She is the Mystery, she is that Rose.
In the Gardens of God, in the daylight divine
I shall come home to thee, Mother of mine.

Is Mary that Rose, then? Mary, the Tree?
But the Blossom, the Blossom there, who can it be?
Who can her Rose be? It could be but One:
Christ Jesus, our Lord – her God and her Son.
  In the Gardens of God, in the daylight divine
  Shew me thy Son, Mother, Mother of mine.

What was the colour of that Blossom bright!
White to begin with, immaculate white.
But what a wild flush on the flakes of it stood,
When the Rose ran in crimsonings down the Cross-wood,
  In the Gardens of God, in the daylight divine
  I shall worship the Wounds with thee, Mother of mine.

How many leaves had it? Five they were then,
Five like the senses, and members of men;
Five is the number by nature, but now
They multiply, multiply, who can tell how.
  In the Gardens of God, in the daylight divine
  Make me a leaf in thee, Mother of mine.

Does it smell sweet, too, in that holy place?
Sweet unto God, and the sweetness is grace;
The breath of it bathes the great heaven above,
In grace that is charity, grace that is love.
  To thy breast, to thy rest, to thy glory divine
  Draw me by charity, Mother of mine.

Gerard Manley Hopkins (1844–89)

That Holy Thing

They all were looking for a king
To slay their foes and lift them high:
Thou cam'st, a little baby thing
That made a woman cry.

O Son of Man, to right my lot
Naught but Thy presence can avail;
Yet on the road Thy wheels are not,
Nor on the sea Thy sail!

My how or when Thou wilt not heed,
But come down Thine own secret stair,
That Thou mayst answer all my need –
Yea, every bygone prayer.

George MacDonald (1824–1905)

Our Lady

Mother of God! no lady thou:
Common woman of common earth!
Our Lady ladies call thee now,
But Christ was never of gentle birth;
A common man of the common earth.

For God's ways are not as our ways.
The noblest lady in the land
Would have given up half her days,
Would have cut off her right hand,
To bear the child that was God of the land.

Never a lady did He choose,
Only a maid of low degree,
So humble she might not refuse
The carpenter of Galilee.
A daughter of the people, she.

Out she sang the song of her heart.
Never a lady so had sung.
She knew no letters, had no art;
To all mankind, in woman's tongue,
Hath Israelitish Mary sung.

And still for men to come she sings,
Nor shall her singing pass away.
'He hath filled the hungry with good things' –
Oh, listen, lords and ladies gay! –
'And the rich He hath sent empty away.'

Mary E. Coleridge (1861–1907)

Unto Us a Son is Given

Given, not lent,
And not withdrawn – once sent,
This Infant of mankind, this One,
Is still the little welcome Son.

New every year,
New born and newly dear,
He comes with tidings and a song,
The ages long, the ages long;

Even as the cold
Keen winter grows not old,
As childhood is so fresh, foreseen,
And spring in the familiar green.

Sudden as sweet
Come the expected feet.
All joy is young, and new all art,
And he, too, whom we have by heart.

Alice Meynell (1847–1922)

A *Meditation for Christmas*

Consider, O my soul, what morn is this!
  Whereon the eternal Lord of all things made,
For us, poor mortals, and our endless bliss,
  Came down from heaven; and, in a manger laid,
  The first, rich, offerings of our ransom paid:
Consider, O my soul, what morn is this!

Consider what estate of fearful woe
  Had then been ours, had He refused this birth;
From sin to sin toss'd vainly to and fro,
  Hell's playthings, o'er a doom'd and helpless earth!
  Had He from us withheld His priceless worth,
Consider man's estate of fearful woe!

Consider to what joys He bids thee rise,
  Who comes, Himself, life's bitter cup to drain!
Ah! look on this sweet Child, whose innocent eyes,
  Ere all be done, shall close in mortal pain,
  That thou at last Love's Kingdom may'st attain:
Consider to what joys He bids thee rise!

Consider all this wonder, O my soul;
  And in thine inmost shrine make music sweet!
Yea, let the world, from furthest pole to pole,
  Join in thy praises this dread birth to greet;
  Kneeling to kiss thy Saviour's infant feet!
Consider all this wonder, O my soul!

Selwyn Image (1849–1936)

The House of Christmas

There fared a mother driven forth
    Out of an inn to roam;
In the place where she was homeless
    All men are at home.
The crazy stable close at hand,
With shaking timber and shifting sand,
Grew a stronger thing to abide and stand
    Than the square stones of Rome.

For men are homesick in their homes,
    And strangers under the sun,
And they lay their heads in a foreign land
    Whenever the day is done.
Here we have battle and blazing eyes,
And chance and honour and high surprise,
But our homes are under miraculous skies
    Where the yule tale was begun.

A child in a foul stable,
    Where the beasts feed and foam;
Only where He was homeless
    Are you and I at home;
We have hands that fashion and heads that know,
But our hearts we lost – how long ago! –
In a place no chart nor ship can show
    Under the sky's dome.

This world is wild as an old wives' tale,
    And strange the plain things are,
The earth is enough and the air is enough
    For our wonder and our war;
But our rest is as far as the fire-drake swings,
And our peace is put in impossible things
Where clashed and thundered unthinkable wings
    Round an incredible star.

To an open house in the evening
    Home shall men come,
To an older place than Eden
    And a taller town than Rome;

To the end of the way of the wandering star,
To the things that cannot be and that are,
To the place where God was homeless
    And all men are at home.

G.K. Chesterton (1874–1936)

Star Silver

The silver of one star
Plays cross-lights against pine green.

And the play of this silver
crosswise against the green
Is an old story...
            thousands of years.

And sheep raisers on the hills by night
Watching the wooly four-footed ramblers,
Watching a single silver star –
Why does the story never wear out?

And a baby slung in a feed-box
Back in a barn in a Bethlehem slum,
A baby's first cry mixing with the crunch
Of a mule's teeth on Bethlehem Christmas corn,
Baby fists softer than snowflakes of Norway,
The vagabond Mother of Christ,
The vagabond men of wisdom,
All in a barn on a winter night,
And a baby there in swaddling clothes on hay –
Why does the story never wear out?

The sheen of it all
Is a star silver and a pine green
For the heart of a child asking a story,
The red and hungry, red and hankering heart
Calling for cross-lights of silver and green.

Carl Sandburg (1878–1967)

At the Manger Mary Sings

O shut your bright eyes that mine must endanger
With their watchfulness; protected by its shade
Escape from my care: what can you discover
From my tender look but how to be afraid?
Love can but confirm the more it would deny.
  Close your bright eye.

Sleep. What have you learned from the womb that bore you
But an anxiety your Father cannot feel?
Sleep. What will the flesh that I gave do for you,
Or my mother love, but tempt you from his will?
Why was I chosen to teach his Son to weep?
  Little One, sleep.

Dream. In human dreams earth ascends to Heaven
Where no one need pray nor ever feel alone.
In your first few hours of life here, O have you
Chosen already what death must be your own?
How soon will you start on the Sorrowful Way?
  Dream while you may.

W.H. Auden (1907–73)

Mother and Child

Holding in clear hands
The world's true light
She lifts its perfect flame
Against the night.

About its pulse of fire
Earth and seas run,
Season and moon and star,
The unruly sun.

Upon the hill a scuffed
Thinness of snow,
First of green thorn, a stream
Stopped in its flow.

She keeps within her hand
The careful day
Now the slow wound of night
Has bled away:

Vivid upon her tongue
Unspoken prayers
That she may not outlive
The life she bears.

Charles Causley (1917–)

The Sheep on Blackening Fields

The sheep on blackening fields
No weather-warning know
As the thin, sapping sun
Annihilates the snow.
Winter has eased its grip,
The struck fountain flows;
Burns in its lamp of leaves
The white flame of the rose.

In the sharp river's gut
Fish and blurred stars unfreeze;
Unclench at the moor's side
The fists of trees.
Unscientifically housed
And in his hand a stone,
Grizzles in dusty hay
A naked child, alone.

A star of bitter red
Above the mountain crest
Writes on the squalling dark,
Christus natus est.
Silently we renew
The ruined bread and wine;
Take the huge-bellied child
Whose flesh is yours, is mine.

Charles Causley (1917–)

Ballad of the Bread Man

Mary stood in the kitchen
    Baking a loaf of bread.
An angel flew in through the window.
    'We've a job for you,' he said.

'God in his big gold heaven,
    Sitting in his big blue chair,
Wanted a mother for his little son.
    Suddenly saw you there.'

Mary shook and trembled,
    'It isn't true what you say.'
'Don't say that,' said the angel.
    'The baby's on its way.'

Joseph was in the workshop
    Planing a piece of wood.
'The old man's past it,' the neighbours said.
    'That girl's been up to no good.'

'And who was that elegant fellow,'
    They said, 'in the shiny gear?'
The things they said about Gabriel
    Were hardly fit to hear.

Mary never answered,
    Mary never replied.
She kept the information,
    Like the baby, safe inside.

It was election winter.
    They went to vote in town.
When Mary found her time had come
    The hotels let her down.

The baby was born in an annexe
    Next to the local pub.
At midnight, a delegation
    Turned up from the Farmers' Club.

They talked about an explosion
    That made a hole in the sky,
Said they'd been sent to the Lamb & Flag
    To see God come down from on high.

A few days later a bishop
    And a five-star general were seen
With the head of an African country
    In a bullet-proof limousine.

'We've come,' they said, 'with tokens
    For the little boy to choose.'
Told the tale about war and peace
    In the television news.

After them came the soldiers
    With rifle and bomb and gun,
Looking for enemies of the state.
    The family had packed and gone.

When they got back to the village
    The neighbours said, to a man,
'That boy will never be one of us,
    Though he does what he blessed well can.'

He went round to all the people
    A paper crown on his head.
Here is some bread from my father.
    Take, eat, he said.

Nobody seemed very hungry.
    Nobody seemed to care.
Nobody saw the god in himself
    Quietly standing there.

He finished up in the papers.
    He came to a very bad end.
He was charged with bringing the living to life.
    No man was that prisoner's friend.

There's only one kind of punishment
    To fit that kind of a crime.
They rigged a trial and shot him dead.
    They were only just in time.

They lifted the young man by the leg,
    They lifted him by the arm,
They locked him in a cathedral
    In case he came to harm.

They stored him safe as water
    Under seven rocks.
One Sunday morning he burst out
    Like a jack-in-the-box.

Through the town he went walking.
    He showed them the holes in his head.
Now do you want any loaves? he cried.
    'Not today,' they said.

Charles Causley (1917–)

From: The Adoration of the Magi

It was the arrival of the kings
that caught us unawares;
we'd looked in on the woman in the barn,
curiosity you could call it,
something to do on a cold winter's night;
we'd wished her well –
that was the best we could do, she was in pain,
and the next thing we knew
she was lying on the straw
– the little there was of it –
and there was this baby in her arms.

It was, as I say, the kings
that caught us unawares...
Women have babies every day,
not that we are there –
let's call it a common occurrence though,
giving birth. But kings
appearing in a stable with a
'Is this the place?' and kneeling,
each with his gift held out towards the child!

They didn't even notice us.
Their robes trailed on the floor,
rich, lined robes that money couldn't buy.
What must this child be
to bring kings from distant lands
with costly incense and gold?
What could a tiny baby make of that?

And what were we to make of –
was it angels falling through the air,
entwined and falling as if from the rafters
to where the gaze of the kings met the child's
– assuming the child could see?
What would the mother do with the gift?
What would become of the child?
And we'll never admit there are angels

or that somewhere between
one man's eyes and another's
is a holy place, a space where a king could be
at one with a naked child,
at one with an astonished soldier.

Christopher Pilling (1936–)

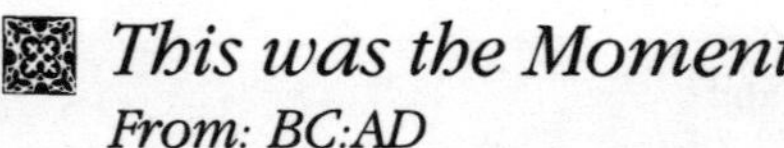

This was the Moment
From: BC:AD

This was the moment when Before
Turned into After, and the future's
Uninvented timekeepers presented arms.

This was the moment when nothing
Happened. Only dull peace
Sprawled boringly over the earth.

This was the moment when even energetic Romans
Could find nothing better to do
Than counting heads in remote provinces.

And this was the moment
When a few farm workers and three
Members of an obscure Persian sect
Walked haphazard by starlight straight
Into the kingdom of heaven.

U.A. Fanthorpe (1929–)

Animal Nativity

The Iliad of peace began
when this girl agreed.
Now goats in trees, fish in the valley
suddenly feel vivid.

Swallows flit in the stable as if
a hatchling of their kind,
turned human, cried in the manger
showing the hunger-diamond.

Cattle are content that this calf
must come in human form.
Spiders discern a water-walker.
Even humans will sense the lamb,

He who frees from the old poem
turtle-dove and snake
who gets death forgiven
who puts the apple back.

Dogs, less enslaved but as starving
as the poorest humans there
crouch, agog as a crux of presence
remembered as a star.

Les Murray (20th century)

two

Teacher and Healer

'A Deep, but Dazzling Darkness'

While the poets of the Middle Ages sung of the birth of Jesus to Mary, or reflected on the cruelty and agony of his death, it is to the poets of much later times that we have to turn to find any substantial interest in his adult life – his years as a Teacher and Healer, the story of Jesus of Nazareth. In fact, of the twenty poems in this section, only three were written before the nineteenth century, and none before the seventeenth. It may be that the miracles and parables of our Lord's brief earthly ministry were well-enough known to earlier ages, but regarded as less momentous, less significant, than the great events of his birth and death. Or it may be that, in an age when the miraculous was commonplace (every saint's bones could do the trick), the miracles of Jesus were not as distinctive or definitive as later ages saw them to be.

Whatever the reason, there are simply fewer poems to choose from! Yet in some ways they make up in quality – in imagination, connection, intuition – what they may lack in quantity. The Jesus of history became a sought-after figure in the nineteenth century, as a more sceptical age questioned the ancient gospel records. The poets, typically, are on a more elusive quest. What does it all *mean*? They are not very bothered with *how* Jesus turned water into wine – the subjects of the first and last poems in this section – but fascinated by its implications. Why did Jesus do it? What does it mean, what does it tell us about material things, about enjoyment and fulfilment and richness of experience?

For Seamus Heaney it mirrors the miracle that the wedding celebrated: the eventual 'consecration' of new life in the bride's womb. What a daring, fascinating connection! Crashaw, writing 300 years earlier, draws a different, but equally daring connection – the evil work of Christ's 'foe' in taking the innocent joy of wine and turning it into the 'wrath and strife' of excess. When the poet is at work, one is never quite sure where the imagination will settle – but seldom on the question 'how', which concerns neither Heaney nor Crashaw.

Neither does it concern the New Zealander, R.A.K. Mason, when he elaborates on that strange remark of Jesus to his mother on the same occasion, the wedding at Cana of Galilee: 'What concern is that to me? My hour is not yet come.' For him, this connects with the great disconnection, the severing of child from mother, the loneliness of the dedicated man who must pursue his path:

even in despite
of her who brought me in pain from her womb,
whose blood made me, who used to bring the light
and sit on the bed up in my little room
and tell me stories and tuck me up at night.

There is a poignancy here that speaks volumes about the humanity of Jesus, the awful cost of obedience, the price of dedication.

It's interesting that three of these poems are about the raising of Lazarus – by Tennyson, Browning and the American Daniel Berrigan. Again, their interest is not in the credibility of the event, but in its implications. For Tennyson, struggling to come to terms with a deep personal bereavement – the death of a young friend – it represents the ultimate hope. He shares the intense, amazed joy of Mary, the sister of Lazarus:

Nor other thought her mind admits
But, he was dead, and there he sits,
And he that brought him back is there.

For Browning, creating an imaginary letter relating the 'strange medical experience of Karshish' – the raising of Lazarus – the interest is in two things. Firstly, there is the human reluctance to accept the miraculous – the witness must be mad. The second is the thought that, if this story were true, then 'the All-Great, were the All-Loving too'. The story speaks not only of eternal power, in other words, but of eternal love.

For Daniel Berrigan, the story is an exercise in the power of tears – the tears of Mary for her brother and the tears of Jesus for his friend ('Jesus wept'):

what, what do tears say to him?

what did he say in tears, that his grief fall
scalding my hands, that cold hands sprung
sleep like a manacle, and drew my eyes a space
that had seen God, back to his human face?

The poems in this section cover a kaleidoscope of images from the gospels: the child Jesus asking questions in the Temple (Sandburg, Knight), the human Jesus, touching the poor and outcast (Thompson, Kavanagh), the Jesus of the temptation, holding communion with the strange animals of the wilderness (Robert Graves), and James Kirkup's vivid picture of the scene at the Last Supper ('Cena'). There are pictures of lives invaded, changed, turned upside down (Sansom, Countee Cullen, Quarles – with his brilliant, sharp, funny sketch of Zaccheus). There is Chesterton's famous donkey, revelling in his fifteen minutes of fame. And there is a chilling poem by the Jamaican, Vivian Virtue, applying the dreadful warning of Jesus about the abuse of children to the waifs of the 'heedless street':

Ragged, unkempt, uncouth,
Orphaned of joy and youth.

And there is Henry Vaughan, whose metaphysical voice picks up one of the great gospel moments of insight, the night-time visit of Nicodemus, a 'ruler of the Jews', to the young rabbi Jesus.

Wise *Nicodemus* saw such light
As made him know his God by night.

Vaughan envies the Jewish seeker. At night all is still:

Dear night! this world's defeat;
The stop to busie fools; cares check and curb;
The day of Spirits; my souls calm retreat
Which none disturb!

But his day *is* disturbed – 'living where the Sun / Doth all things wake, and where all mix and tyre / themselves'. And then, with the leap of imagination that marks the great poet, he draws his lesson:

There is in God (some say)
A deep, but dazzling darkness; As men here
Say it is late and dusky, because they
    See not all clear.
O for that night! where I in him
Might live invisible and dim.

Perhaps it is that 'deep, but dazzling darkness' that makes even the human Jesus so elusive to the poetic imagination – 'they / See not all clear…' Or perhaps, as Carl Sandburg suggests, echoing the words of Jesus, it is that we cannot see clearly because we have lost the child's eye of faith. There are questions – questions that baffle the 'old men' – that are 'Found in the eyes of children alone…'

On Zacheus

Me thinks, I see, with what a busie hast,
Zacheus climb'd the Tree: But, O, how fast,
How full of speed, canst thou imagine (when
Our *Saviour* call'd) he powder'd downe agen!
He ne're made tryall, if the boughs were sound,
Or rotten; nor how far 'twas to the ground:
There was no danger fear'd; At such a Call,
Hee'l venture nothing, that dare feare a fall;
Needs must hee downe, by such a *Spirit* driven;
Nor could he fall, unlesse he fell to *Heaven*:
Downe came *Zacheus*, ravisht from the Tree;
Bird that was shot ne're dropt so quicke as he.

Francis Quarles (1592–1644)

To our Lord, upon the Water made Wine

Thou water turn'st to Wine (faire friend of Life).
    Thy foe to crosse the sweet Arts of thy Reigne
Distills from thence the Teares of wrath and strife,
    And so turnes wine to Water backe againe.

Richard Crashaw (1612–49)

The Night
(John 3:2)

Through the pure *Virgin-shrine*,
That sacred vail drawn o'er thy glorious noon
That men may look and live as Glo-worms shine,
And face the Moon:
Wise *Nicodemus* saw such light
As made him know his God by night.

Most blest believer he!
Who in that land of darkness and blinde eyes
Thy long expected healing wings could see,
When thou didst rise,
And what can never more be done,
Did at midnight speak with the Sun!

O who will tell me, where
He found thee at that dead and silent hour!
What hallowed solitary ground did bear
So rare a flower,
Within whose sacred leafs did lie
The fulness of the Deity.

No mercy-seat of gold,
No dead and dusty *Cherub*, nor carv'd stone,
But his own living works did my Lord hold
And lodge alone;
Where *trees and herbs* did watch and peep
And wonder, while the *Jews* did sleep.

Dear night! this worlds defeat;
The stop to busie fools; cares check and curb;
The day of Spirits; my souls calm retreat
Which none disturb!
Christs progress, and his prayer time;
The hoirs to which high Heaven doth chime.

Gods silent, searching flight:
When my Lords head is fill'd with dew, and all
His locks are wet with the clear drops of night;
His still, soft call;
His knocking time; the souls dumb watch,
When Spirits their fair kindred catch.

Were all my loud, evil days
Calm and unhaunted as is thy dark Tent,
Whose peace but by some *Angels* wing or voice
Is seldom rent;
Then I in heaven all the long year
Would keep, and never wander here.

But living where the Sun
Doth all things wake, and where all mix and tyre
Themselves and others, I consent and run
To ev'ry myre,
And by this worlds ill-guiding light,
Erre more than I can do by night.

There is in God (some say)
A deep, but dazzling darkness; As men here
Say it is late and dusky, because they
See not all clear.
O for that night! where I in him
Might live invisible and dim.

Henry Vaughan (1622–95)

The Healer

To a Young Physician, with Doré's Picture of Christ Healing the Sick

So stood of old the holy Christ
    Amidst the suffering throng;
With whom His lightest touch sufficed
    To make the weakest strong.

That healing gift He lends to them
    Who use it in His name;
The power that filled His garment's hem
    Is evermore the same.

For lo! in human hearts unseen
    The Healer dwelleth still,
And they who make His temples clean
    The best subserve His will.

The holiest task by Heaven decreed,
    An errand all divine,
The burden of our common need
    To render less is thine.

The paths of pain are thine. Go forth
    With patience, trust, and hope;
The sufferings of a sin-sick earth
    Shall give thee ample scope.

Beside the unveiled mysteries
    Of life and death go stand,
With guarded lips and reverent eyes
    And pure of heart and hand.

So shalt thou be with power endued
    From Him who went about
The Syrian hillsides doing good,
    And casting demons out.

That Good Physician liveth yet
    Thy friend and guide to be;
The Healer by Gennesaret
    Shall walk the rounds with thee.

John Greenleaf Whittier (1807–92)

From: In Memoriam

When Lazarus left his charnel-cave,
And home to Mary's house return'd,
Was this demanded – if he yearn'd
To hear her weeping by his grave?

'Where wert thou, brother, those four days?'
There lives no record of reply,
Which telling what it is to die
Had surely added praise to praise.

From every house the neighbours met,
The streets were fill'd with joyful sound,
A solemn gladness even crown'd
The purple brows of Olivet.

Behold a man raised up by Christ!
The rest remaineth unreveal'd;
He told it not; or something seal'd
The lips of that Evangelist.

Her eyes are homes of silent prayer,
Nor other thought her mind admits
But, he was dead, and there he sits,
And he that brought him back is there.

Then one deep love doth supersede
All other, when her ardent gaze
Roves from the living brother's face,
And rests upon the Life indeed.

All subtle thought, all curious fears,
Borne down by gladness so complete,
She bows, she bathes the Saviour's feet
With costly spikenard and with tears.

Thrice blest whose lives are faithful prayers,
Whose loves in higher love endure;
What souls possess themselves so pure,
Or is there blessedness like theirs?

Alfred, Lord Tennyson (1809–92)

From: An Epistle Containing the Strange Medical Experience of Karshish

Thou wilt object – why have I not ere this
Sought out the sage himself, the Nazarene
Who wrought this cure, enquiring at the source,
Conferring with the frankness that befits?
Alas! It grieveth me, the learned leech
Perished in a tumult many years ago,
Accused – our learning's fate – of wizardry.
Rebellion, to the setting up a rule
And creed prodigious as described to me.
His death which happened when the earthquake fell
(Prefiguring, as soon appeared, the loss
To occult learning in our lord the sage
That lived there in the pyramid alone)
Was wrought by the mad people – that's their wont –
On vain recourse, as I conjecture it,
To his tried virtue, for miraculous help –
How could he stop the earthquake? That's their way!
The other imputations must be lies:
But take one – though I loathe to give it thee,
In mere respect to any good man's fame!
(And after all our patient Lazarus
Is stark mad – should we count on what he says?
Perhaps not – though in writing to a leech
'Tis well to keep back nothing of a case.)
This man so cured regards the curer then,
As – God forgive me – who but God himself,
Creater and Sustainer of the world,
That came and dwelt in flesh on it awhile!
– 'Sayeth that such an One was born and lived,
Taught, healed the sick, broke bread at his own house,
Then died, with Lazarus by, for ought I know,
And yet was… what I said nor choose repeat,
And must have so avouched himself, in fact,
In hearing of this very Lazarus
Who saith – but why all this of what he saith?
Why write of trivial matters, things of price
Calling at every moment for remark?

I noticed on the margin of a pool
Blue-flowering borage, the Aleppo sort,
Aboundeth, very nitrous. It is strange!

Thy pardon for this long and tedious case,
Which, now that I review it, needs must seem
Unduly dwelt on, prolixly set forth.
Nor I myself discern in what is writ
Good cause for the peculiar interest
And awe indeed this man has touched me with.
Perhaps the journey's end, the weariness
Had wrought upon me first. I met him thus –
I crossed a ridge of short sharp broken hills
Like an old lion's cheek-teeth. Out there came
A moon made like a face with certain spots
Multiform, manifold, and menacing:
Then a wind rose behind me. So we met
In this old sleepy town at unaware,
The man and I. I send thee what is writ.
Regard it as a chance, a matter risked
To this ambiguous Syrian – he may lose,
Or steal, or give it thee with equal good.
Jerusalem's repose shall make amends
For time this letter wastes, thy time and mine,
Till when, once more thy pardon and farewell!

The very God! think, Abib; dost thou think?
So, the All-Great, were the All-Loving too –
So, through the thunder comes a human voice
Saying, 'O heart I made, a heart beats here!
Face, my hands fashioned, see it in myself.
Thou hast no power nor may'st conceive of mine,
But love I gave thee, with Myself to love,
And thou must love me who have died for thee!'
The madman saith He said so: it is strange.

Robert Browning (1812–89)

In No Strange Land

'The Kingdom of God is Within You.'

O World invisible, we view thee,
O world intangible, we touch thee,
O world unknowable, we know thee,
Inapprehensible, we clutch thee!

Does the fish soar to find the ocean,
The eagle plunge to find the air –
That we ask of the stars in motion
If they have rumour of thee there?

Not where the wheeling systems darken,
And our benumb'd conceiving soars! –
The drift of pinions, would we hearken,
Beats at our own clay-shutter'd doors.

The angels keep their ancient places; –
Turn but a stone, and start a wing!
'Tis ye, 'tis your estrangèd faces,
That miss the many-splendour'd thing.

But (when so sad thou canst not sadder)
Cry; – and upon thy so sore loss
Shall shine the traffic of Jacob's ladder
Pitched betwixt Heaven and Charing Cross.

Yea, in the night, my Soul, my daughter,
Cry, – clinging Heaven by the hems;
And lo, Christ walking on the water,
Not of Gennesareth, but Thames!

Francis Thompson (1859–1907)

The Donkey

When fishes flew and forests walked
  And figs grew upon thorn,
Some moment when the moon was blood
  Then surely I was born.

With monstrous head and sickening cry
  And ears like errant wings,
The devil's walking parody
  On all four-footed things.

The tattered outlaw of the earth,
  Of ancient crooked will;
Starve, scourge, deride me: I am dumb,
  I keep my secret still.

Fools! For I also had my hour;
  One far fierce hour and sweet:
There was a shout about my ears,
  And palms before my feet.

G.K. Chesterton (1874–1936)

Child

The young child, Christ, is straight and wise
And asks questions of the old men, questions
Found under running water for all children
And found under shadows thrown on still waters
By tall trees looking downward, old and gnarled.
Found to the eyes of children alone, untold,
Singing a low song in the loneliness.

Carl Sandburg (1878–1967)

In The Wilderness

Christ of His gentleness
Thirsting and hungering
Walked in the wilderness;
Soft words of grace He spoke
Unto lost desert-folk
That listened wondering.
He heard the bitterns call
From ruined palace-wall,
Answered them brotherly.
He held communion
With the she-pelican
Of lonely piety.
Basilisk, cockatrice,
Flocked to His homilies,
With mail of dread device,
With monstrous barbèd stings.
With eager dragon-eyes;
Great rats on leather wings,
And poor blind broken things,
Foul in their miseries.
And ever with Him went,
Of all His wanderings
Comrade, with ragged coat,
Gaunt ribs – poor innocent –
Bleeding foot, burning throat,
The guileless old scape-goat;
For forty nights and days
Followed in Jesus' ways,
Sure guard behind Him kept,
Tears like a lover wept.

Robert Graves (1895–1935)

Cena

A crowded Last
Supper, thirteen heads,
Twenty-six hands, some
Under the table's
Long linenfold skirts,
Elbows getting in the way,
Feet in sandals kicked
Under the stout trestles,
Fingers dipped in dishes,
Breaking bread, carafe
Decanting acid wine,
Dark, muddy, poor stuff,
John, James, Judas,
Even the betrayer
His face tanned by a golden halo
Turned all in profile
And the thirteen auras
All at different heights
Bob and jostle above
The tablecloth's white Jordan
Like balloons, buoys, mooring lights.

In mid-channel
One full face
In solitude.

James Kirkup (1912–)

Street Corner Christ

I saw Christ today
At a street corner stand,
In the rags of a beggar he stood
He held ballads in his hand.

He was crying out: 'Two for a penny
Will anyone buy
The finest ballads ever made
From the stuff of joy?'

But the blind and deaf went past
Knowing only there
An uncouth ballad seller
With tail-matted hair.

And I whom men call fool
His ballads bought,
Found Him whom the pieties
Have vainly sought.

Patrick Kavanagh (1904–67)

Footnote to John ii 4

Don't throw your arms around me in that way:
I know that what you tell me is the truth –
yes I suppose I loved you in my youth
as boys do love their mothers, so they say,
but all that's gone from me this many a day:
I am a merciless cactus an uncouth
wild goat a jagged old spear the grim tooth
of a lone crag… Woman I cannot stay.

Each one of us must do his work of doom
and I shall do it even in despite
of her who brought me in pain from her womb,
whose blood made me, who used to bring the light
and sit on the bed up in my little room
and tell me stories and tuck me up at night.

R.A.K. Mason (1905–71)

Lazarus

Sister, you placed my heart in its stone room
where no flowers curiously come, and sun's voice
rebuffed, hangs on the stones dumb. What I could not bear
I still must hear. Why do your tears fall?

why does their falling move him, the friend, the
unsuspected lightning: that he walk our garden
with no flowers upon his friend, but a voice splitting
my stone to a dream gone, my sleep

to day? what, what do tears say to him?

what did he say in tears, that his grief fall
scalding my hands, that cold hands sprung
sleep like a manacle, and drew my eyes a space
that had seen God, back to his human face?

Daniel Berrigan (20th century)

Mary of Magdala

Bruised were my breasts with the weight of men,
    Uncounted men,
Unknown before and in an hour
    Unknown again:

Bruised my brain by each loveless love,
    Each casual thrust;
My spirit lying corrupted, foul,
    In its tomb of lust.

He found me, raised me like Lazarus
    From that living grave,
Showed me I still had a self to honour,
    A soul to save.

I wiped my lips and bound my hair,
    And to men's surprise
No longer walked through the Street of Doves
    With sidelong eyes.

I was a woman once more – delivered
    From a second birth,
Possessed by none but God and he
    In the whole earth.

Oh, oil and tears were little to pay –
    Nor a heart riven –
For the wealth of his love, his giving love,
    And the grace of heaven.

Clive Sansom (1910–81)

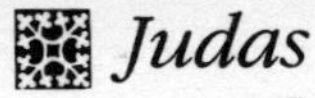

Judas

You don't understand, Levi,
  Nobody understands
How the sight of his face haunts me,
  The shape of his hands.

I remember the light on his face
  When he first called me,
My mind immured from doubt
  As his hands enwalled me.

Why, in the name of his God,
  Did it have to cease?
Why sometimes that fervour returned,
  Never that peace?

I gave up more than they,
  Those net-menders;
Yet always reserved for them
  Were the throne and its splendours.

I had more faith than they.
  Not prophecies –
I'd have planted his Kingdom here
  Where God's temple is.

Clive Sansom (1910–81)

Simon the Cyrenian Speaks

He never spoke a word to me,
    And yet he called my name;
He never gave a sign to me,
    And yet I knew and came.

At first I said 'I will not bear
    His cross upon my back;
He only seeks to place it there,
    Because my skin is black.'

But he was dying for a dream,
    And he was very meek,
And in His eyes there shone a gleam
    Men journey far to seek.

It was Himself my pity bought;
    I did for Christ alone
What all of Rome could not have wrought
    With bruise of lash or stone.

Countee Cullen (1903–46)

Waifs

They shout no stranger, troublous news
Along the heedless street
Than wrongs their own loud page abuse,
The starveling waifs who cannot choose
But barter soul for bread:
Ragged, unkempt, uncouth,
Orphaned of joy and youth.

And yet their Nazarene Brother said,
Who had not where to lay His head,
Their angels in the highest place
Always behold the Father's face.

Nomads without a tribe or name,
Wild Ishmaels of the street,
They wander, whom Crime waits to claim…
Upon the highways of our shame
How urgently they spread
The warnings of our doom
Who still deny them room!

For better on our necks, said He,
A mill-stone and the swallowing sea,
Than to be cause of least offence
To one young spirit's innocence.

Vivian Virtue (1911–)

Father to the Man

I warned the parents, you know,
when he was a child. I said

This boy must really not be allowed
to argue about the law with lawyers and about God
with theologians. And he seems, I said,
to fancy himself as a doctor, too. At this rate
we shall have him, perhaps, giving water
to a feverish patient. Little thinking
he'd do just that; and was lucky
the lad recovered.

It will come to no good, I said.
But one gets no thanks.

And so it went on
until, later, we lost touch;
for he was away for some years,
no one knew where.

Afterwards, I admit, I was half convinced. More than half,
I suppose I should say.

When he preached – and I shall hear no such sermons again –
it seemed that immutable right and wrong –
no, it was not that their boundaries changed. But somehow
acts and facts seemed with a shake of a word
to fall – I saw such a toy once, of foolish beads –
in a different pattern. What was done was the same,
and right and wrong were the same, and yet
not the same, being done in a different world.

There was a wedding, for instance,
with, in plain Aramaic, too much drink,
and you know the country customs –
I fear the old Gods are by no means dead.
Well, he was there, and he preached on the sabbath,
and spoke, just in passing, about the wedding;

and, you know, these junketings (to call them no worse)
seemed transformed, seemed a part
(like David's dancing in the Temple)
of our holy religion; and,
what was stranger, our religion
seemed to have grown, and to be our life.

Well, you see, it has come to no good,
as I told his parents, children
must listen, and lawful authority speak.

… and yet
this is the saddest news… and I
am nearer to death…

John Knight (1906–)

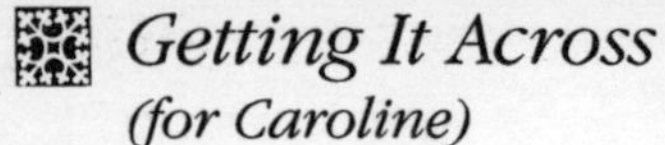

Getting It Across
(for Caroline)

'His disciples said unto him, Lo, now speakest thou plainly, and speakest no proverb. Now are we sure that thou knowest all things.'
John 16:29–30

This is the hard thing.
Not being God, the Son of Man,
– I was born for that part –
But patiently incising on these yokel faces,
Mystified, bored and mortal,
The vital mnemonics they never remember.

There is enough of Man in my God
For me to construe their frowns. I feel
The jaw-cracking yawns they try to hide
When out I come with one of my old
Chestnuts. *Christ! not that bloody*
Sower again, they are saying, or *God!*
*Not the Prodigal f***ing Son.*
Give us a new one, for Messiah's sake.

They know my unknowable parables as well
As each other's shaggy dog stories.
I say! I say! I say! There was this Samaritan,
This Philistine and this Roman… or
What did the high priest say
To the belly dancer? All they need
Is the cue for laughs. My sheep and goats,
Virgins, pigs, figtrees, loaves and lepers
Confuse them. Fishing, whether for fish or men,
Has unfitted them for analogy.

Yet these are my mouths. Through them only
Can I speak with Augustine, Aquinas, Martin, Paul,
Regius Professors of Divinity,
And you, and you.
How can I cram the sense of Heaven's kingdom
Into our pidgin-Aramaic quayside jargon?

I envy Moses, who could choose
The diuturnity of stone for waymarks
Between man and Me. He broke the tablets,
Of course. I too know the easy messages
Are the ones not worth transmitting;
But he could at least carve.
The prophets too, however luckless
Their lives and instructions, inscribed on wood,
Papyrus, walls, their jaundiced oracles.

I alone must write on flesh. Not even
The congenial face of my Baptist cousin,
My crooked affinity Judas, who understands,
Men who would give me accurately to the unborn
As if I were something simple, like bread.
But Pete, with his headband stuffed with fishhooks,
His gift for rushing in where angels wouldn't,
Tom, for whom metaphor is anathema,
And James and John, who want the room at the top –
These numskulls are my medium. I called them.

I am tattooing God on their makeshift lives.
My Keystone Cops of disciples, always
Running absurdly away, or lying ineptly,
Cutting off ears and falling into the water,
These Sancho Panzas must tread my Quixote life,
Dying ridiculous and undignified,
Flayed and stoned and crucified upside down.
They are the dear, the human, the dense, for whom
My message is. That might, had I not touched them,
Have died decent respectable upright deaths in bed.

U.A. Fanthorpe (1929–)

Cana Revisited

No round-shouldered pitchers here, no stewards
To supervise consumption or supplies
And water locked behind the taps implies
No expectation of miraculous words.

But in the bone-hooped womb, rising like yeast,
Virtue intact is waiting to be shown,
The consecration wondrous (being their own)
As when the water reddened at the feast.

Seamus Heaney (1939–)

three

The Mystery of the Cross

Exploring the Deepmost

No act in human history can be more widely recognized than the crucifixion of Jesus. From a hundred million crucifixes, on church walls and hung on gold round people's necks, the tortured figure of a man looks down at us. Thorns bring blood from his scalp, nails bring it from his hands and feet. This single, pain-racked figure is the symbol and sign of Christianity, its true distinguishing mark. The world is still full of gods, but none like this. As Edward Shillito's poem in this section concludes: 'And not a god has wounds but Thou alone.' It is a strange and terrible uniqueness, which has fascinated, appalled and inspired poets down the centuries.

Once again, there is a distinction between the way in which poets of different periods have explored the 'mystery of the cross'. While the early poets, shaped by the Catholic culture of the middle ages, celebrated the crucifixion as the way of salvation – 'Tell them with words this is the tree of glory' – they were also appalled by the physical suffering of Christ:

> Blood spilt over whiteness wide,
> From the wounded body crucified.

It was this paradox – between the ugliness of the deed and the generosity of its consequences – that absorbed the poetic imagination. Even Shakespeare, whose religious beliefs seem to be shrouded in conscious reticence, returns to this theme. And, typically, expresses it with powerful and memorable economy:

> Why, all the souls that were were forfeit once;
> And he that might the vantage best have took
> Found out the remedy. (*Measure for Measure*)

It was the metaphysical poets of the next century who turned their attention to the cross in terms of its impact on the individual mind, heart and conscience. For them it was much more than a theological concept, or even a means of salvation. Christ on the cross challenged their values, put all the other concerns of life into perspective. Here is John Donne, 'riding westward' on Good Friday 1613:

> Though these things, as I ride, be from mine eye,
> They are present yet to my memory,

For that looks towards them; and thou look'st towards me,
O Saviour, as thou hang'st upon the tree.

And William Alabaster, 'Upon the Ensignes of Christes Crucifyinge', calls the crucified Christ to deal with the consequences of his sin – 'no sinne like mine', he says:

Take up the tarte Spunge of thy Passion
And blot it forth...

The poets of the eighteenth century – here, Dryden and Pope – treat the cross to theological analysis rather than celebration or awe, as befitted an era of cool rationalism, though Pope manages to lift the language of classical hymnody to something approaching personal emotion. Perhaps there is a strain here of the Roman Catholic faith to which he clung throughout his life.

We have to wait until the nineteenth century, typically, for the first real notes of scepticism or questioning to arise. Swinburne's powerful poem 'Before a Crucifix', looks into the 'hidden face of man', over which 'the years have woven a viewless veil':

If thou wast verily man's lover,
What did thy love or blood avail?

For him, it had been a pointless sacrifice. He contrasts the 'carrion crucified' of the cross with the sickening history of the Church:

... seeing against thy side,
Too foul to speak of or to see,
The leprous likeness of a bride...

Strangely enough, a twentieth-century poet, Jack Clemo, in his poem 'The Winds', uses the same analogy of the Church as the 'bride' of Christ, but more positively, to claim that, though one of the branches of the tree bears 'the Crucified',

... all the other branches bear
The choice fruits of the Bride.

For Oscar Wilde, undergoing in Reading Gaol the appalling experience of the hanging of a fellow prisoner, the cross offers comfort. After all, it was a condemned man who called on the dying Lord for mercy, and was promised that he would that day join him in Paradise:

And he of the swollen purple throat,
And the stark and staring eyes,

Waits for the holy hands that took
    The Thief to Paradise...

Wilde died, at the age of forty-six, in the first year of the twentieth century. Strangely, in a period when Christianity in the English-speaking world has generally been regarded as in decline, this century was to see many poets turning back to the 'mystery of the cross' for clues to the suffering, violence and bloodshed that have been its hallmarks. Edward Shillito, writing during the appalling slaughter of the First World War, addressed the figure on the cross:

We know today what wounds are, have no fear,
    Show us Thy Scars, we know the countersign.

F.T. Prince was an army officer in the Second World War. His powerful poem 'Soldiers bathing' arose out of watching his men bathing naked in the sea, 'their flesh worn by the trade of war'. That contrast provided for him, he says, 'indirectly or directly a commentary / On the Crucifixion'.

    And the picture burns
With indignation and pity and despair by turns,
Because it is the obverse of the scene
Where Christ hangs murdered, stripped, upon the Cross...

Time and again the modern poets wrestle with this same paradox. For R.S. Thomas, 'There is no meaning in life,/ unless men can be found to reject / love.' So,

    God needs his martyrdom.
The mild eyes stare from the Cross
in perverse triumph.

This is a long way from the language of the early poets, or even of Donne and Alabaster, but it has a painful honesty about it. The cross is a contradiction – in the apostle Paul's words, 'a stumbling-block to Jews and foolishness to the Gentiles'. How could the death of one man, even the Son of God, wipe clean the sin and evil of human history? And how could an event of such ugliness produce the beauty of forgiveness? Yet poetry thrives on paradox, and perhaps the poets can help us where theologians may struggle.

When the poet laureate, Ted Hughes, had to write a poem to mark the funeral in August 1997 of Diana, Princess of Wales, it was to the cross that he turned for a key to understanding the violent death of a young woman who had spent her last years in a struggle to outlaw the random violence of the land-mine. He captured it in a single couplet:

> Love is broken on the Cross
> The Flower on the Gun.

And it was to the cross, indeed to the traditional scene of the *pieta*, Mary holding across her knees the broken body of her Son, that C. Day Lewis turned for imagery to respond to one of the most appalling events in twentieth-century history, the assassination of President Kennedy. The President's wife, Jackie, cradled his body on the back seat of the car, evoking for Lewis the image of Mary:

> A divine, dazed compassion calms her features.
> She holds all earth's dead sons upon her lap.

The Awesome Mystery

I have called this section 'The Mystery of the Cross', not because I think the idea of the cross is in itself beyond human understanding, but because it is beyond human analysis. There are many theories and doctrines of the atonement. Scholars have wrestled with the nature of the sacrifice of Christ and with ideas like expiation and propitiation. But when all has been said and done, this is the *mysterium tremendum*, the awesome mystery of eternal love. As such, it is, perhaps, better experienced, celebrated, explored, welcomed, than wholly understood. That is the path to the cross which the poets have trod, and which they invite us to join.

Because human life is inextricably bound up with the twin mysteries of suffering and love, of inexpressible joy and indescribable loss, we are never nearer the heart of things than we are as we approach the cross of Christ. In truth, this is what life is like: ugly and beautiful; full of hatred, full of love; a strange amalgam of birth and death, hope and fear, joy and sorrow. Nothing expresses that essential paradox more completely than the suffering and death of the Son of God. Alice Meynell caught it beautifully in her poem 'The Crucifixion':

> Oh, man's capacity
> For spiritual sorrow, corporal pain!
> Who has explored the deepmost of that sea,
> With heavy links of a far-fathoming chain?…

One only has explored
The deepmost; but he did not die of it.
Not yet, not yet he died. Man's human Lord
Touched the extreme; it is not infinite.

The Dream of the Rood

Listen! I will describe the best of dreams
which I dreamed in the middle of the night
when, far and wide, all men slept.
It seemed that I saw a wondrous tree
soaring into the air, surrounded by light,
the brightest of crosses; that emblem was entirely
cased in gold; beautiful jewels
were strewn around its foot, just as five
studded the cross-beam. All the angels of God,
fair creations, guarded it. That was no cross
of a criminal, but holy spirits and men on earth
watched over it there – the whole glorious universe...

Now I command you, my loved man,
to describe your vision to all men;
tell them with words this is the tree of glory
on which the Son of God suffered once
for the many sins committed by mankind,
and for Adam's wickedness long ago.
He sipped the drink of death. Yet the Lord rose
with His great strength to deliver man.
Then He ascended into heaven. The Lord Himself,
Almighty God, with His host of angels,
will come to the middle-world again
on Domesday to reckon with each man.
Then He who has the power of judgement
will judge each man just as he deserves
for the way in which he lived this fleeting life.
No-one then will be unafraid
as to what words the Lord will utter.

Anonymous (9th century?),
translated by Kevin Crossley-Holland

You, who Created Everything

You, who created everything,
Sweet Father and our heavenly King,
Hear, as I, your Son, implore:
For Man this flesh and blood I bore.

Bright and clear my breast and side,
Till blood spilt over whiteness wide,
From the wounded body crucified.

Stiff and stark my long arms rise,
Dimness and darkness shroud my eyes;
And like cold marble hang my thighs.

My feet are red with flowing blood,
Their holes are washed through with that flood.
Mercy on human sin, Father above!
My wounds cry out to you in love.

Anonymous (14th century),
translated by David Winter

From: Measure for Measure
Isabella and Angelo, Act 2

Angelo:
Your brother is a forfeit of the law,
And you but waste your words.

Isabella:
Alas! Alas!
Why, all the souls that were were forfeit once;
And he that might the vantage best have took
Found out the remedy. How would you be
If He, which is the top of judgment, should
But judge you as you are? O, think on that:
And mercy then will breathe within your lips,
Like man new made.

William Shakespeare (1564–1616)

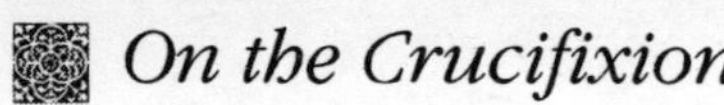

On the Crucifixion

It was but now their sounding clamours sung,
Blessed is he, that comes from the most high,
And all the mountains with Hosanna rung,
And now, away with him, away they cry,
And nothing can be heard but crucify:
    It was but now, the crown itself they save,
    And golden name of king unto him gave,
And now, no king, but only Caesar, they will have:

It was but now they gathered blooming May,
And of his arms disrob'd the branching tree,
To strew with boughs, and blossoms all thy way,
And now, the branchless trunk a cross for thee,
And May, dismayed, thy coronet must be:
    It was but now they were so kind, to throw
    Their own best garments, where thy feet should go,
And now, thyself they strip, and bleeding wounds they show.

See where the author of all life is dying:
O fearful day! he dead, what hope of living?
See where the hopes of all our lives are buying:
O cheerful day! they bought, what fear of grieving?

Giles Fletcher (1588–1623)

Good Friday, 1613, Riding Westward

Let man's soul be a sphere, and then, in this,
The intelligence that moves, devotion is,
And as the other Spheres, by being grown
Subject to foreign motions, lose their own,
And being by others hurried every day,
Scarce in a year their natural form obey:
Pleasure or business, so, our souls admit
For their first mover, and are whirl'd by it.
Hence is't, that I am carried towards the west
This day, when my soul's form bends toward the east.
There I should see a sun, by rising set,
And by that setting endless day beget;
But that Christ on this cross, did rise and fall,
Sin had eternally benighted all.
Yet dare I almost be glad, I do not see
That spectacle of too much weight for me.
Who sees God's face, that is self life, must die;
What a death were it then to see God die?
It made his own lieutenant, Nature, shrink,
It made his footstool crack, and the sun wink.
Could I behold those hands which span the poles,
And turn all spheres at once, pierced with those holes?
Could I behold that endless height which is
Zenith to us, and our Antipodes,
Humbled below us? or that blood which is
The seat of all our souls, if not of his,
Made dirt of dust, or that flesh which was worn
By God, for his apparel, ragg'd and torn?
If on these things I durst not look, durst I
Upon his miserable mother cast mine eye,
Who was God's partner here, and furnished thus
Half of that sacrifice, which ransomed us?
Though these things, as I ride, be from mine eye,
They are present yet to my memory,
For that looks towards them; and thou look'st towards me,
O Saviour, as thou hang'st upon the tree;
I turn my back to thee, but to receive
Corrections, till thy mercies bid thee leave.

O think me worth thine anger, punish me,
Burn off my rusts, and my deformity,
Restore thine image, so much, by thy grace,
That thou may'st know me, and I'll turn my face.

John Donne (1572–1631)

Upon the Ensignes of Christes Crucifyinge

O sweete and bitter monuments of paine,
Bitter to Christ who all the paine endur'd,
But sweete to mee, whose Death my life procur'd,
How shall I full express, such loss, such gaine.
My tongue shall bee my Penne, mine eyes shall raine
Teares for my Inke, the Cross where I was cur'd
Shall be my Booke, where having all abjur'd
And calling heavens to record in that plaine
Thus plainely will I write: *no sinne like mine*.
When I have done, doe thou Jesu divine
Take up the tarte Spunge of thy Passion
And blot it forth: then bee thy spirit the Quill,
Thy bloode the Inke, and with compassion
Write thus upon my soule: *thy Jesus still*.

William Alabaster (1567–1640)

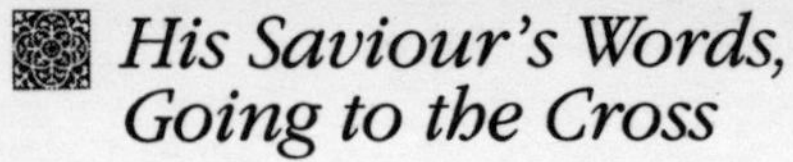

His Saviour's Words, Going to the Cross

Have, have ye no regard, all ye
Who pass this way, to pity me
Who am a man of misery?

A man both bruis'd, and broke, and one
Who suffers not here for mine own
But for my friends' transgression?

Ah! Sion's Daughters, do not fear
The Cross, the Cords, the Nails, the Spear,
The Myrrh, the Gall, the Vinegar,

For Christ, your loving Saviour, hath
Drunk up the wine of God's fierce wrath;
Only, there's left a little froth,

Less for to taste, than for to shew
What bitter cups had been your due,
Had He not drank them up for you.

Robert Herrick (1591–1674)

Christ Crucified

Thy restless feet now cannot go
　　For us and our eternal good,
As they were ever wont. What though
　　Thy swim, alas! in their own flood?

Thy hands to give thou canst not lift,
　　Yet will thy hand still giving be;
It gives, but O, itself's the gift!
　　It gives tho' bound, tho' bound 'tis free!

Richard Crashaw (1612–49)

Most Blessed Vine

　　Most blessed Vine!
　　Whose juice so good
　　I feel as wine,
But thy fair branches felt as blood;
　　How wert thou pressed
　　To be my feast!
　　In what deep anguish
　　Didst thou languish,
What springs of sweat and blood did drown thee!
　　How in one path
　　Did the full wrath
　　Of thy great Father
　　Crowd and gather,
Doubling thy griefs, when none would own thee!

Henry Vaughan (1622–95)

From: Religio Laici

Thus Man by his own strength to Heaven would soar:
And would not be obliged to God for more.
Vain, wretched creature, how art thou misled
To think thy Wit these God-like notions bred!
These truths are not the product of thy mind,
But dropped from Heaven, and of a nobler kind.
Revealed religion first informed thy sight,
And *Reason* saw not till *Faith* sprung the light.
Hence all thy Natural Worship takes the source:
'Tis *Revelation* what thou thinkst *Discourse*.

But if there be a *Power* too just and strong
To wink at crimes and bear unpunished wrong,
Look humbly upward, see his will disclose
The forfeit first, and then the fine impose,
A mulct thy poverty could never pay
Had not eternal wisdom found the way
And with cœlestial wealth supplied thy store;
His justice makes the fine, his mercy quits the score.
See God descending in thy human frame;
The offended, suffering in the offender's name.
All thy misdeeds to Him imputed see,
And all His righteousness devolved on thee.

John Dryden (1631–1700)

Hymn

Thou art my God, sole object of my love;
Not for the hope of endless joys above;
Not for the fear of endless pains below,
Which they who love thee not must undergo.
For me, and such as me, thou deign'st to bear
An ignominious cross, the nails, the spear:
A thorny crown transpierced thy sacred brow,
While bloody sweats from every member flow.
For me in tortures thou resign'st thy breath,
Embraced me on the cross, and saved me by thy death.
And can these sufferings fail my heart to move?
What but thyself can now deserve my love?
Such as then was, and is, thy love to me,
Such is, and shall be still, my love to thee –
To thee, Redeemer! Mercy's sacred spring!
My God, my Father, Maker, and my King!

Alexander Pope (1688–1744)

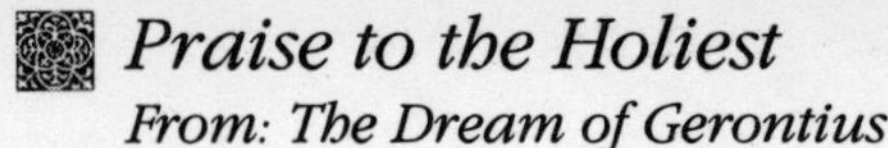

Praise to the Holiest

From: The Dream of Gerontius

Praise to the Holiest in the height,
And in the depth be praise,
In all his words most wonderful,
Most sure in all his ways.

O loving wisdom of our God!
When all was sin and shame,
A second Adam to the fight
And to the rescue came.

O wisest love! that flesh and blood,
Which did in Adam fail,
Should strive afresh against the foe,
Should strive and should prevail;

And that a higher gift than grace
Should flesh and blood refine,
God's presence and his very self,
And essence all divine.

O generous love! that he who smote
In Man for man the foe,
The double agony in Man
For man should undergo;

And in the garden secretly,
And on the cross on high,
Should teach his brethren, and inspire
To suffer and to die.

Praise to the Holiest in the height,
And in the depth be praise,
In all his words most wonderful,
Most sure in all his ways.

John Henry Newman (1801–90)

Good Friday

Am I a stone, and not a sheep,
    That I can stand, O Christ, beneath Thy cross,
    To number drop by drop Thy Blood's slow loss,
And yet not weep?

Not so those women loved
    Who with exceeding grief lamented Thee;
    Not so fallen Peter weeping bitterly;
Not so the thief was moved;

Not so the Sun and Moon
    Which hid their faces in a starless sky,
    A horror of great darkness at broad noon –
I, only I.

Yet give not o'er,
    But seek Thy sheep, true Shepherd of the flock;
    Greater than Moses, turn and look once more
And smite a rock.

Christina Rossetti (1830–94)

Before a Crucifix

O hidden face of man, whereover
    The years have woven a viewless veil,
If thou wast verily man's lover,
    What did thy love or blood avail?
Thy blood the priests make poison of,
And in gold shekels coin thy love.

So when our souls look back to thee
    They sicken, seeing against thy side,
Too foul to speak of or to see,
    The leprous likeness of a bride,
Whose kissing lips through his lips grown
Leave their God rotten to the bone.

When we would see thee man, and know
    What heart thou hadst toward men indeed,
Lo, thy blood-blackened altars; lo,
    The lips of priests that pray and feed
While their own hell's worm curls and licks
The poison of the crucifix.

Thou bad'st let children come to thee;
    What children now but curses come?
What manhood in that God can be
    Who sees their worship, and is dumb?
No soul that lived, loved, wrought, and died,
Is this their carrion crucified.

Nay, if their God and thou be one,
    If thou and this thing be the same,
Thou shouldst not look upon the sun;
    The sun grows haggard at thy name.
Come down, be done with, cease, give o'er;
Hide thyself, strive not, be no more.

Algernon Charles Swinburne (1837–1909)

From: Christmas Antiphones

Thou the word and Lord
    In all time and space
Heard, beheld, adored,
With all ages poured
    Forth before thy face,

Lord, what worth in earth
    Drew thee down to die?
What therein was worth,
Lord, thy death and birth?
    What beneath thy sky?

Light above all love
    By thy love was lit,
And brought down the Dove
Feathered from above
    With the wings of it.

Algernon Charles Swinburne (1837–1909)

The Crucifixion

Oh, man's capacity
For spiritual sorrow, corporal pain!
Who has explored the deepmost of that sea,
With heavy links of a far-fathoming chain?

That melancholy lead,
Let down in guilty and in innocent hold,
Yet into childish hands deliverèd,
Leaves the sequestered floor unreached, untold.

One only has explored
The deepmost; but he did not die of it.
Not yet, not yet he died. Man's human Lord
Touched the extreme; it is not infinite.

But over the abyss
Of God's capacity for woe he stayed
One hesitating hour; what gulf was this?
Forsaken he went down, and was afraid.

Alice Meynell (1847–1922)

The Passion

O most exceeding bitter cry,
From ashen lips in anguish curled!
O body that on Calvary
    The sword of death devours!
    O river red that pours,
And winds a bloody bandage round the wounded world!

O cup they made to overflow,
Whereat our Saviour drinks his fill!
O crown upon that piteous brow,
    With scarlet buds of scorn
    Amid the twisted thorn!
O bloody passion-rose upon the sanguine hill!

Christ with a rod hath broke the bands,
And shattered Death; and lo, the rod
Hath pierced and bruised His holy hands,
    Come hither, ye that mourn,
    And see what He hath borne;
Behold the purple wound within the breast of God.

Andrew Young (1885–1971)

From: The Ballad of Reading Gaol

And thus we rust Life's iron chain
    Degraded and alone:
And some men curse, and some men weep,
    And some men make no moan:
But God's eternal Laws are kind
    And break the heart of stone.

And every human heart that breaks,
    In prison-cell or yard,
Is as that broken box that gave
    Its treasure to the Lord,
And filled the unclean leper's house
    With the scent of costliest nard.

Ah! Happy they whose hearts can break
    And peace of pardon win!
How else may man make straight his plan
    And cleanse his soul from Sin?
How else but through a broken heart
    May Lord Christ enter in?

And he of the swollen purple throat,
    And the stark and staring eyes,
Waits for the holy hands that took
    The Thief to Paradise;
And a broken and a contrite heart
    The Lord will not despise.

The man in red who reads the Law
    Gave him three weeks of life,
Three little weeks in which to heal
    His soul of his soul's strife,
And cleanse from every blot of blood
    The hand that held the knife.

And with tears of blood he cleansed the hand,
    The hand that held the steel:
For only blood can wipe out blood,
    And only tears can heal:
And the crimson stain that was of Cain
    Became Christ's snow-white seal.

Oscar Wilde (1854–1900)

The Happy Tree

There was a bright and happy tree;
The wind with music laced its boughs:
Thither across the houseless sea
Came singing birds to house.

Men grudged the tree its happy eves,
Its happy dawns of eager sound;
So all that crown and tower of leaves
They levelled with the ground.

They made an upright of the stem,
A cross-piece of a bough they made:
No shadow of their deed on them
The fallen branches laid.

But blithely, since the year was young,
When they a fitting hill did find,
There on the happy tree they hung
The Saviour of mankind.

Gerald Gould (1885–1936)

Ballad of the Goodly Fere

Simon Zelotes speaketh it somewhile after the Crucifixion

Ha' we lost the goodliest fere o' all
For the priests and the gallows-tree?
Aye, lover he was of brawny men,
O' ships and the open sea.

When they came wi' a host to take Our Man
His smile was good to see,
'First let these go!' quo' our Goodly Fere,
'Or I'll see ye damned,' says he.

Aye, he sent us out through the crossed high spears,
And the scorn of his laugh rang free,
'Why took ye not me when I walked about
Alone in the town?' says he.

Oh, we drank his 'Hale' in the good red wine
When we last made company,
No capon priest was the Goodly Fere
But a man o' men was he.

I ha' seen him drive a hundred men
Wi' a bundle o' cords swung free,
When they took the high and holy house
For their pawn and treasury.

They'll no get him a' in a book I think
Though they write it cunningly;
No mouse of the scrolls was the Goodly Fere
But aye loved the open sea.

If they think they ha' snared our Goodly Fere
They are fools to the last degree.
'I'll go to the feast,' quo' our Goodly Fere,
'Though I go to the gallows-tree.'

'Ye ha' seen me heal the lame and the blind,
And wake the dead,' says he,
'Ye shall see one thing to master all:
'Tis how a brave man dies on the tree.'

A son of God was the Goodly Fere
That bade us his brothers be.
I ha' seen him cow a thousand men.
I ha' seen him upon the tree.

He cried no cry when they drave the nails
And the blood gushed hot and free,
The hounds of the crimson sky gave tongue
But never a cry cried he.

I ha' seen him cow a thousand men
On the hills o' Galilee,
They whined as he walked out calm between,
Wi' his eyes like the grey o' the sea.

Like the sea that brooks no voyaging
With the winds unleashed and free,
Like the sea that he cowed at Gennesaret
Wi' twey words spoke' suddenly.

A master of men was the Goodly Fere,
A mate of the wind and sea,
If they think they ha' slain our Goodly Fere
They are fools eternally.

I ha' seen him eat o' the honeycomb
Sin' they nailed him to the tree.

Ezra Pound (1885–1972)

Fere: Companion, mate

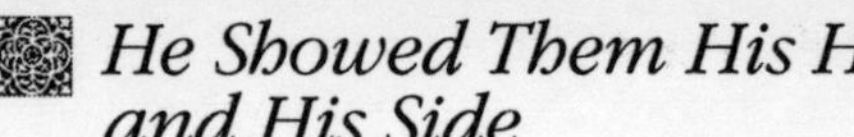

He Showed Them His Hands and His Side

If we have never sought, we seek Thee now;
    Thine eyes burn through the dark, our only stars;
We must have sight of thorn-pricks on Thy brow,
    We must have Thee, O Jesus of the Scars.

The heavens frighten us; they are too calm;
    In all the universe we have no place.
Our wounds are hurting us, where is Thy balm?
    Lord Jesus by Thy Scars, we claim Thy grace.

If when the doors are shut, Thou drawest near,
    Only reveal Thine hands, that side of Thine;
We know today what wounds are, have no fear,
    Show us Thy Scars, we know the countersign.

The other gods were strong: but Thou wast weak:
    They rode, but Thou didst stumble to a throne;
But to our wounds only God's wounds can speak,
    And not a god has wounds but Thou alone.

Edward Shillito (1872–1948)

He is the Lonely Greatness

He is the lonely greatness of the world –
    (His eyes are dim).
His power it is holds up the Cross
    That holds up Him.

He takes the sorrow of the threefold hour –
    (His eyelids close).
Round Him and round, the wind – His Spirit – where
    It listeth blows.

And so the wounded greatness of the world
    In silence lies –
And death is shattered by the light from out
    Those darkened eyes.

Madeleine Caron Rock (20th century)

Soldiers Bathing

The sea at evening moves across the sand.
Under a reddening sky I watch the freedom of a band
Of soldiers who belong to me. Stripped bare
For bathing in the sea, they shout and run in the warm air;
Their flesh worn by the trade of war, revives
And my mind towards the meaning of it strives.

All's pathos now. The body that was gross,
Rank, ravenous, disgusting in the act or in repose,
All fever, filth and sweat, its bestial strength
And bestial decay, by pain and labour grows at length
Fragile and luminous. 'Poor bare forked animal,'
Conscious of his desires and needs and flesh that rise and fall,
Stands in the soft air, tasting after toil
The sweetnes of his nakedness: letting the sea-waves coil
Their frothy tongues about his feet, forgets
His hatred of the war, its terrible pressure that begets
A machinery of death and slavery,
Each being a slave and making slaves of others: finds that he
Remembers his old freedom in a game
Mocking himself, and comically mimics fear and shame.

He plays with death and animality;
And reading in the shadows of his pallid flesh, I see
The idea of Michelangelo's cartoon
Of soldiers bathing, breaking off before they were half done
At some sortie of the enemy, an episode
Of the Pisan wars with Florence. I remember how he showed
Their muscular limbs that clamber from the water,
And heads that turn across the shoulder, eager for the slaughter,
Forgetful of their bodies that are bare,
And hot to buckle on and use the weapons lying there.
– And I think too of the theme another found
When, shadowing men's bodies on a sinister red ground,
Another Florentine, Pollaiuolo,
Painted a naked battle: warriors, straddled, hacked the foe,
Dug their bare toes into the ground and slew
The brother-naked man who lay between their feet and drew
His lips back from his teeth in a grimace.

They were Italians who knew war's sorrow and disgrace
And showed the thing suspended, stripped: a theme
Born out of the experience of war's horrible extreme
Beneath a sky where even the air flows
With lacrimae Christi. For that rage, that bitterness, those blows,
That hatred of the slain, what could they be
But indirectly or directly a commentary
On the Crucifixion? And the picture burns
With indignation and pity and despair by turns,
Because it is the obverse of the scene
Where Christ hangs murdered, stripped, upon the Cross. I mean,
That is the explanation of its rage.

And we too have our bitterness and pity that engage
Blood, spirit, in this war. But night begins,
Night of the mind: who nowadays is conscious of our sins?
Though every human deed concerns our blood,
And even we must know, what nobody has understood,
That some great love is over all we do,
And that is what has driven us to this fury, for so few
Can suffer all the terror of that love:
The terror of that love has set us spinning in this groove
Greased with our blood.

These dry themselves and dress,
Combing their hair, forget the fear and shame of nakedness.
Because to love is frightening we prefer
The freedom of our crimes. Yet, as I drink the dusky air,
I feel a strange delight that fills me full,
Strange gratitude, as if evil itself were beautiful,
And kiss the wound in thought, while in the west
I watch a streak of red that might have issued from Christ's breast.

F.T. Prince (1912–)

The Winds

There is a tree grows upside down,
    Its roots are in the sky;
Its lower branches reach the earth
    When amorous winds are nigh.

On one lone bough there starkly hangs
    A Man just crucified,
And all the other branches bear
    The choice fruits of the Bride.

When Pleasure's wind goes frisking past,
    Unhallowed by a prayer,
It swirls dead leaves from earth-born trees,
    Old growths of pride and care.

The gracious fruits are hidden by
    These leaves of human stain;
The Crucified, beneath his load
    Shudders, as if in pain.

But swift springs down a credal wind,
    It thrills through all the boughs;
The dead leaves scatter and are lost;
    The Christ renews his vows.

His hands direct the Spirit's wind
    Branch after branch to shake;
The Bride's fruit drops, and at the touch
    Elected hearts awake.

Jack Clemo (1916–94)

Emblems of the Passion

Here, you said, the voice well-bred
Carried in that classic head,
Unremarking, as your fashion,
That the slipping sky was ashen,
Are the Emblems of the Passion.

Overhead a heeling bird
Struck on the split sky the word,
But I do not think you heard
As the blood of the last sun
On the wounded water spun.

Safe beneath a shooting spire
Here you waded the green wire
Of the graveyard's fallen fire,
Dreams, desires, as fish asleep
In the silence of its deep.

On the raging wood, unread
Histories of the hanged, the dead
Searched the cyphers of my head:
Soldier, seamless robe on rail,
Hyssop, hammer, crown and nail.

From the forest of my fears
Thirty-coined, a tree of tears
Flowered on the sour, slab floor
By the high, the holy door
Of death's strict and silent shore.

Hand with scourges, hand with spear,
Lantern, ladder, cross and gear,
Cock on pillar. Chaste and clear
God's trapping tongue: *Consider this*
Head of Judas, and the kiss.

Underneath that seamless sky
Stripped, I met your startled eye
Saw your sweating lip, and I
Whose face was Judas, felt you start
At the rivers of the heart.

Charles Causley (1917–)

Amen

It was all arranged:
the virgin with child, the birth
in Bethlehem, the arid journey uphill
to Jerusalem. The prophets foretold
it, the scriptures conditioned him
to accept it. Judas went to his work
with his sour kiss; what else
could he do?

A wise old age,
the honours awarded for lasting,
are not for a saviour. He had
to be killed; salvation acquired
by an increased guilt. The tree,
with its roots in the mind's dark,
was divinely planted, the original fork
in existence. There is no meaning in life,
unless men can be found to reject
love. God needs his martyrdom.
The mild eyes stare from the Cross
in perverse triumph. What does he care
that the people's offerings are so small?

R.S. Thomas (1913–)

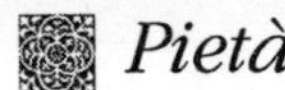

Pietà

Written on the Assassination of President John F. Kennedy

Naked, he sags across her cumbered knees.
Heavy and beautiful like the child she once
Aroused from sleep, to fall asleep on the next breath.

The passion is done,
But death has not yet stiffened him against her,
Nor chilled the stripling grace into a dogma.
For a timeless hour, imagined out of marble,
He comes back to his mother, he is all
And only hers.

And it is she whom death has magnified
To bear the burden of his flesh – the arms
Excruciated no more, the gash wiped clean.
A divine, dazed compassion calms her features.
She holds all earth's dead sons upon her lap.

In the triumphal car
Closely escorted through the gaze and heart of
A city, at the height of his golden heyday,
He suddenly slumps.

Cameras show her bending to shelter him
(But death has moved faster), and then a pink
Nimbus veiling the exploded skull.

No order here, no artistry, except for
The well-drilled wounds, the accomplished sacrifice.
But from that wreck
Two living images are saved – the wife who
Nurses a shattered world in her lap;

And, flying the coffin home, refuses to change
Out of her yellow, blood-spattered dress, with
'Let them all see what was done to him.'

C. Day Lewis (1904–72)

On the Death of Diana, Princess of Wales

Mankind is many rivers
That only want to run.
Holy Tragedy and Loss
Make the many One.
Mankind is a Holy, crowned
Mother and her Son.
For worship, for mourning:
God is here, is gone.
Love is broken on the Cross
The Flower on the Gun.

Ted Hughes (1930–)

four

Resurrection

If something very remarkable had not happened after the execution of Jesus it is doubtful if anyone would be writing poems about him nearly 2,000 years later. That, in a word, is the significance of the resurrection. Putting it as objectively as I can, the followers of Jesus became convinced that he was still alive and had appeared to them: not as a ghost, but as himself, body, mind and spirit. They believed it, and they were prepared to die for that belief. And it was that utter, unshakeable conviction that carried the infant Church through its early years of ridicule and persecution to the point at which the 'pale Galilean' had triumphed and the whole Roman empire had fallen under his spell.

So the resurrection was and is crucial to Christianity. Indeed, without it, there is no such thing. The apostle Paul put it very starkly: 'If Christ has not been raised, your faith is futile.'

Yet 'The Resurrection' is the shortest section of this anthology, simply because there are fewer poems about it. The cross, as we have seen, has offered profound and luminous images for poets old and new. So has the story of Christ's birth, and so, as we shall see, has the question of his person and meaning. But the resurrection – so utterly fundamental to the Christian faith – has left even the dreamers of dreams speechless.

But not, thankfully, all of them! On the whole, it is the believers among the poets who have been moved to reflect on this most mysterious of all mysteries. They have explored the resurrection as victory (over death, evil, sin and injustice), as the transformation of humanity, as a bright light in the darkness of mortality. If death is the greatest cause of human sorrow, then victory over death must be the greatest cause of human joy. In many of these poems, that joy is celebrated with the confidence of faith, especially in the earlier poets, and by later ones with the tentative, intuitive reticence that is so deep a mark of modern poetry.

Victory is the theme of several of the early poems:

The great victor again is risen on high,
That for our quarrel to the death was wounded;
The sun that waxed all pale now shines out bright,
And darkness cleared, our faith is now refounded.

So writes William Dunbar in the fifteenth century – I have modernized the language here, though not in the full, anthology version. A century later, Spenser could sound equally triumphant:

Most glorious Lord of life, that on this day
Didst make thy triumph over death and sin;
And, having harrowed hell, didst bring away
Captivity thence captive, us to win…

Milton, in *Paradise Lost*, sets this theme of triumph in the exalted language of the seventeenth century:

Death his death's wound shall then receive, and stoop
Inglorious, of his mortal sting disarmed;
I through the ample air in triumph high
Shall lead Hell captive maugre Hell, and show
The powers of darkness bound.

Henry Vaughan is rather more curt:

Death and darkness get you packing,
Nothing now to man is lacking.

Resurrection as Transformation

Two centuries later, that first of the truly 'modern' poets, Gerard Manley Hopkins, celebrated a victory through the resurrection, but a far more elusive one: the transformation of human nature. The language is complex, full of daring metaphor, but the message is persuasive. Christ was the 'Manshape, that shone', but 'death blots black out'.

… Enough! the Resurrection,
A heart's-clarion! Away grief's gasping,
joyless days, dejection.

And its consequence?

In a flash, at a trumpet crash,
I am all at once what Christ is, since he was what I am, and
This Jack, joke, poor potsherd, patch, matchwood,
immortal diamond,
Is immortal diamond.

I suppose that is 'triumphant', in one sense. It certainly celebrates a victory. But for Hopkins the impact of the resurrection is in its significance for humanity: a new destiny, sharing the risen life of the resurrected one, transformed from 'mortal trash' into 'immortal diamond'.

Another Christian poet of this century, Christina Rossetti, saw the same process in the linkage of Easter and Spring:

Out in the rain a world is growing green,
  On half the trees quick buds are seen
    Where glued-up buds have been.
Out in the rain God's Acre stretches green,
  Its harvest quick tho' still unseen:
    For there the Life hath been.

And what difference does that 'Life' make?

  ... yea, Christ is risen again:
  Wherefore both life and death grow plain
    To us who wax and wane;
For Christ Who rose shall die no more again:
  Amen: till He makes all things plain
    Let us wax on and wane.

Oscar Wilde's poem 'Easter Day' is not strictly about Easter, but about the contrast between the ornate splendour of the papal procession compared with the poverty and humility of the Jesus of history. Alice Meynell, in what for me is one of the most moving Easter poems, also reflects on the human setting of the death and resurrection of Jesus. The one was public, noisy, clamorous. The other – the event that was of infinite moment – took place in the 'shuttered dark':

And all alone, alone, alone,
He rose again behind the stone.

The poets of the twentieth century, typically, pick up the little things, make the extraordinary connections. For R.S. Thomas it's the garment of Jesus, for which the soldiers gambled:

  ... yet the invisible
garment for which they played
was no longer at stake, but worn
by him in this risen existence.

Like Alice Meynell, he observes the 'absence of clamour', the 'answer must quietly emerge'.

For the Caribbean poet Derek Walcott, the faith he had 'betrayed' was distractingly signalled by the emergence of butterflies from rotting logs – 'stuttering "yes" to the resurrection; "yes, yes is our answer"' – the same analogy that Christina Rossetti made between nature and resurrection, but shaped in a very different way.

In his other poem in the section, 'Easter', Walcott wrestles in a highly imaginative way with the question of the human and divine nature in Christ, and how they connect and disconnect in his death and resurrection. It is in the form of a fable about a black dog, who shadowed his daughter Anna's heel, just as humanity shadowed the life of Jesus, shaping him to the cross, nailing him there:

> Then the shadow slunk away,
> crawling low on its belly,
> and it left there knowing
> that never again
> would He ever need it;
> it reentered the earth,
> it didn't eat for three days,
> it didn't go out...

But that wasn't, of course, the end of the story. It 'peeped out carefully/ like a mole from its hole', emerging into the daylight 'looking for those forms/ that could give back its shape', until:

> it keeps nosing for His shape
> and it finds it again, in
> the white echo of a pigeon
> with its wings extended.

Once again the poets show their ability to tease out truths that are not irrational, but beyond reason. The historic truth of the resurrection is a matter for human consideration and human decision. But the poets draw out for us other levels of meaning, other areas of understanding – levels that go beyond the simple question of whether we do, or do not, believe the 'facts'. And there is nothing new about this. Hopkins' apparently fanciful idea that the resurrection turns 'mortal trash' into 'immortal diamond' is not so far from St Paul's argument that the mortal body is 'sown in dishonour, and raised in glory': 'For the trumpet will sound, and the dead will be raised imperishable, and we will be changed.'

But everything in the end rests on the reality. If the resurrection was just a game with words, or another way of seeing the rebirth of Spring, or simply metaphor or image, then what would be left of the Christian belief in the resurrection of Jesus, or in life beyond death? This is the theme of 'Seven Stanzas at Easter', by the American novelist-poet John Updike:

> Let us not mock God with metaphor,
> analogy, sidestepping, transcendence;
> making of the event a parable, a sign painted in the
> faded credulity of earlier ages:
> let us walk through the door.

 *On the Resurrection of Christ*

Done is a battell on the dragon blak,
Our campioun Chryst confountet hes his force;
The yettis of hell ar brokin with a crak,
The signe triumphall rasit is of the croce,
The divillis trymmillis with hiddous voce,
The saulis ar borrowit and to the blis can go,
Chryst with his blud our ransonis dois indoce:
Surrexit Dominus de sepulchro.

Dungin is the deidly dragon Lucifer,
The crewall serpent with the mortall stang;
The auld kene tegir with his teith on char,
Quhilk in a wait hes lyne for us so lang,
Thinking to grip us in his clows strang;
The merciful Lord wald nocht that it wer so,
He maid him for to felye of that fang:
Surrexit Dominus de sepulchro.

He for our saik that sufferit to be slane,
And lyk a lamb in sacrifice wes dicht,
Is lyk a lyone rissin up agane,
And as gyane raxit him on hicht;
Sprungin is Aurora radius and bright,
On loft is gone the glorious Appollo,
The blisfull day depairtit fro the nycht:
Surrexit Dominus de sepulchro.

The grit victour agane is rissin on hicht,
That for our querrell to the deth was woundit;
The sone that wox all paill now schynis bricht,
And dirknes clerit, our fayth is now refoundit;
The knell of mercy fra the hevin is soundit,
The Cristin ar deliverit of thair wo,
The Jowis and their errour ar confoundit:
Surrexit Dominus de sepulchro.

The fo is chasit, the battell is done ceis,
The presone brokin, the jevellouris fleit and flemit;
The weir is gon, convermit is the peis,
The fetteris lowsit and the dungeoun temit,

The ransoun maid, the presoneris redemit;
The feild is win, our cumin is the fo,
Dispulit of the tresur that he yemit:
Surrexit Dominus de sepulchro.

William Dunbar (1465–1513)

 *Easter Day*

Most glorious Lord of life, that on this day
Didst make thy triumph over death and sin;
And, having harrowed hell, didst bring away
Captivity thence captive, us to win:
This joyous day, dear Lord, with joy begin,
And grant that we, for whom thou diddest die,
Being with thy dear blood clean washed from sin,
May live for ever in felicity;
And that thy love we weighing worthily,
May likewise love thee for the same again;
And for thy sake, that all like dear didst buy,
With love may one another entertain.
    So let us love, dear Love, like as we ought:
    Love is the lesson which the Lord us taught.

Edmund Spenser (1552–99)

Easter Morn

Say, earth, why hast thou got thee new attire,
And stick'st thy habit full of daisies red?
Seems that thou dost to some high thought aspire,
And some new-found-out bridegroom mean'st to wed:
Tell me, ye trees, so fresh apparellèd –
So never let the spiteful canker waste you,
So never let the heavens with lightning blast you –
Why go you now so trimly dressed, or whither haste you?

Answer me, Jordan, why thy crooked tide
So often wanders from his nearest way,
As though some other way thy stream would slide,
And fain salute the place where something lay.
And you, sweet birds that, shaded from the ray,
Sit carolling and piping grief away,
The while the lambs to hear you, dance and play,
Tell me, sweet birds, what is it you so fain would say?

Giles Fletcher (1588–1623)

Easter

I got me flowers to straw Thy way,
I got me boughs off many a tree;
But Thou wast up by break of day,
And brought'st Thy sweets along with Thee.

Yet though my flowers be lost, they say
A heart can never come too late;
Teach it to sing Thy praise this day,
And then this day my life shall date.

George Herbert (1593–1633)

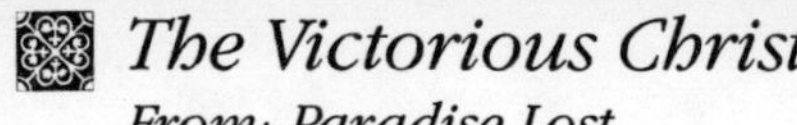

The Victorious Christ
From: Paradise Lost

'Death his death's wound shall then receive, and stoop
Inglorious, of his mortal sting disarmed;
I through the ample air in triumph high
Shall lead Hell captive maugre Hell, and show
The powers of darkness bound. Thou, at the sight
Pleased, out of heaven shalt look down and smile,
While, by Thee raised, I ruin all my foes –
Death last, and with his carcase glut the grave;
Then, with the multitude of My redeemed,
Shall enter Heaven, long absent, and return,
Father, to see Thy face, wherein no cloud
Of anger shall remain, but peace assured
And reconcilement: wrath shall be no more
Thenceforth, but in Thy presence joy entire.'

John Milton (1608–74)

Easter Hymn

Death and darkness get you packing,
Nothing now to man is lacking,
All your triumphs now are ended,
And what Adam marred is mended;
Graves are beds now for the weary,
Death a nap, to wake more merry;
Youth now, full of pious duty,
Seeks in thee for perfect beauty,
The weak, and agèd tired, with length
Of days, from thee look for new strength,
And infants with thy pangs contest
As pleasant, as if with the breast;
Then, unto him, who thus hath thrown
Even to contempt thy kingdom down,
And by his blood did us advance
Unto his own inheritance,
To him be glory, power, praise,
From this, unto the last of days.

Henry Vaughan (1622–95)

Easter Monday

Out in the rain a world is growing green,
    On half the trees quick buds are seen
        Where glued-up buds have been.
Out in the rain God's Acre stretches green,
    Its harvest quick tho' still unseen:
        For there the Life hath been.

If Christ hath died his brethren well may die,
    Sing in the gate of death, lay by
        This life without a sigh:
For Christ hath died and good it is to die;
    To sleep when so He lays us by,
        Then wake without a sigh.

Yes, Christ hath died, yea, Christ is risen again:
    Wherefore both life and death grow plain
        To us who was and wane;
For Christ Who rose shall die no more again:
    Amen: till He makes all things plain
        Let us wax on and wane.

Christina Rossetti (1830–94)

That Nature is a Heraclitean Fire and of the Comfort of the Resurrection

Cloud-puffball, torn tufts, tossed pillows flaunt forth,
then chevy on an air-
built thoroughfare: heaven-roysterers, in gay-gangs
they throng: they glitter in marches.
Down roughcast, down dazzling whitewash, wherever
an elm arches,
Shivelights and shadowtackle in long lashes lace,
lance, and pair.
Delightfully the bright wind boisterous ropes,
wrestles, beats earth bare
Of yestertempest's creases; in pool and rutpeel parches
Squandering ooze to squeezed dough, crust, dust;
stanches, starches
Squadroned masks and manmarks treadmire toil there
Footfretted in it. Million-fuelèd, nature's bonfire
burns on.
But quench her bonniest, dearest to her, her clearest-
selvèd spark
Man, how fast his firedint, his mark on mind, is gone!
Both are in an unfathomable, all is in an enormous dark
Drowned. O pity and indignation! Manshape, that
shone
Sheer off, disseveral, a star, death blots black out; nor mark
Is any of him at all so stark
But vastness blurs and time beats level. Enough! the
Resurrection,
A heart's-clarion! Away grief's gasping, joyless
days, dejection.
Across my foundering deck shone
A beacon, an eternal beam. Flesh fade, and mortal trash
Fall to the residuary worm; world's wildfire, leave but ash:
In a flash, at a trumpet crash,
I am all at once what Christ is, since he was what I am, and
This Jack, joke, poor potsherd, patch, matchwood,
immortal diamond,
Is immortal diamond.

Gerard Manley Hopkins (1844–89)

Easter Day

The silver trumpets rang across the Dome:
    The people knelt upon the ground with awe:
    And borne upon the necks of men I saw,
Like some great God, the Holy Lord of Rome.
Priest-like, he wore a robe more white than foam,
    And, king-like, swathed himself in royal red,
    Three crowns of gold rose high upon his head:
In splendour and in light the Pope passed home.
My heart stole back across wide wastes of years
    To One who wandered by a lonely sea,
    And sought in vain for any place of rest:
    'Foxes have holes, and every bird its nest.
    I, only I, must wander wearily,
    And bruise my feet, and drink wine salt with tears.'

Oscar Wilde (1854–1900)

Easter Night

All night had shout of men and cry
  Of woeful women filled his way;
Until that noon of sombre sky
  On Friday, clamour and display
Smote him; no solitude had he,
  No silence, since Gethsemane.

Public was Death; but Power, but Might,
  But Life again, but Victory,
Were hushed within the dead of night,
  The shuttered dark, the secrecy.
And all alone, alone, alone,
He rose again behind the stone.

Alice Meynell (1847–1922)

Suddenly

As I had always known
he would come, unannounced,
remarkable merely for the absence
of clamour. So truth must appear
to the thinker; so, at a stage
of the experiment, the answer
must quietly emerge. I looked
at him, not with the eye
only, but with the whole
of my being, overflowing with
him as a chalice would
with the sea. Yet was he
no more there than before,
his area occupied
by the unhaloed presences.
You could put your hand
in him without consciousness
of his wounds. The gamblers
at the foot of the unnoticed
cross went on with
their dicing; yet the invisible
garment for which they played
was no longer at stake, but worn
by him in this risen existence.

R.S. Thomas (1913–)

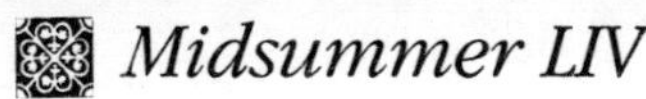

Midsummer LIV

The midsummer sea, the hot pitch road, this grass, these shacks that made me,
jungle and razor grass shimmering by the roadside, the edge of art;
wood lice are humming in the sacred wood,
nothing can burn them out, they are in the blood;
their rose mouths, like cherubs, sing of the slow science
of dying – all heads, with, at each ear, a gauzy wing.
Up at Forest Reserve, before branches break into sea,
I looked through the moving, grassed window and thought 'pines,'
or conifers of some sort. I thought, they must suffer
in this tropical heat with their child's idea of Russia.
Then suddenly, from their rotting logs, distracting signs
of the faith I betrayed, or the faith that betrayed me –
yellow butterflies rising on the road to Valencia
stuttering 'yes' to the resurrection; 'yes, yes is our answer,'
the gold-robed Nunc Dimittis of their certain choir.
Where's my child's hymnbook, the poems edged in gold leaf,
the heaven I worship with no faith in heaven,
as the Word turned toward poetry in its grief?
Ah, bread of life, that only love can leaven!
Ah, Joseph, though no man ever dies in his own country,
the grateful grass will grow thick from his heart.

Derek Walcott (1930–)

Easter

Anna, my daughter,
you have a black dog
that noses your heel,
selfless as a shadow;
here is a fable
about a black dog:
On the last sunrise
the shadow dressed with Him,
it stretched itself also –
they were two big men
with one job to do.
But life had been lent to one
only for this life.
They strode in silence toward
uncontradicting night.
The rats at the Last Supper
shared crumbs with their shadows,
the shadow of the bread
was shared by the bread;
when the candles lowered,
the shadow felt larger,
so He ordered it to leave;
He said where He was going
it would not be needed,
for there there'd be either
radiance or nothing.
It stopped when He turned
and ordered it home,
then it resumed the scent;
it felt itself stretching
as the sun grew small
like the eyes of the soldiers
receding into holes
under the petrified
serpents on their helmets;
the narrowing pupils
glinted like nailheads,
so before He lay back
it crept between the wood

as if it were the pallet
they had always shared;
it crept between the wood
and the flesh nailed to the wood
and it rose like a black flag
as the crossbeam hoisted
itself and the eyes
closed very slowly
extinguishing the shadow –
everything was nothing.
Then the shadow slunk away,
crawling low on its belly,
and it left there knowing
that never again
would He ever need it;
it reentered the earth,
it didn't eat for three days,
it didn't go out,
then it peeped out carefully
like a mole from its hole,
like a wolf after winter,
like a surreptitious serpent,
looking for those forms
that could give back its shape;
then it ran out when the bells began making wide rings
and rings of radiance;
it keeps nosing for His shape
and it finds it again, in
the white echo of a pigeon
with its wings extended
like a shirt on a clothesline,
like a white shirt on Monday
dripping from a clothesline,
like the greeting of a scarecrow
or a man yawning
at the end of a field.

Derek Walcott (1930–)

Seven Stanzas at Easter

Make no mistake: if He rose at all
it was as His body;
if the cells' dissolution did not reverse, the molecules
    reknit, the amino acids rekindle,
the Church will fall.

It was not as the flowers,
each soft Spring recurrent;
it was not as His Spirit in the mouths and fuddled
    eyes of the eleven apostles;
it was as His flesh: ours.

The same hinged thumbs and toes,
the same valved heart
that – pierced – died, withered, paused, and then
    regathered out of enduring Might
new strength to enclose.

Let us not mock God with metaphor,
analogy, sidestepping, transcendence;
making of the event a parable, a sign painted in the
    faded credulity of earlier ages:
let us walk through the door.

The stone is rolled back, not papier-mâché,
not a stone in a story,
but the vast rock of materiality that in the slow
    grinding of time will eclipse for each of us
the wide light of day.

And if we will have an angel at the tomb,
make it a real angel,
weighty with Max Planck's quanta, vivid with hair,
    opaque in the dawn light, robed in real linen
spun on a definite loom.

Let us not seek to make it less monstrous,
for our own convenience, our own sense of beauty,
lest, awakened in one unthinkable hour, we are
    embarrassed by the miracle,
and crushed by remonstrance.

John Updike (1932–)

five

The Christ of Human Experience

'The Low Lintel of the Human Heart'

In the previous four sections the poems have been based around what we might call the 'story' of Jesus – his birth, life, death and resurrection. This section, by some distance the longest in the book, is about the response of human beings to that 'story'. In these poems faith and doubt, mysticism and scepticism, heartfelt longing and intellectual misgiving rub shoulders. This is Jesus as people have *experienced* him – from Swinburne's 'pale Galilean' to Porter's 'master haunter'. It is like a cosmic consulting room, in which the poets congregate to open their souls to us about a person who has, in some way or another, deeply affected how they think and feel.

Many of these poems, of course, are poems of faith – deep and sometimes passionate faith, like Gerard Manley Hopkins', seeing the 'just man' as one who: 'Acts in God's eye what in God's eye he is – Christ.' Or George Herbert, for whom 'Christ is my onely head':

Onely another head
I have, another heart and breast,
Another musick, making live not dead,
Without whom I could have no rest:
In him I am well drest.

Or Edith Sitwell, writing her poem during the air raids on London in 1940, yet seeing even in the horror of human suffering the sacred heart bearing its wounds:

Still falls the Rain –
Still falls the blood from the Starved Man's wounded Side:
He bears in his Heart all wounds – those of the light
that died,
The last faint spark
In the self-murdered heart, the wounds of the sad
uncomprehending dark.

Sometimes faith spills over into mystical experience. Indeed, you may feel that both Hopkins and Sitwell have already crossed that elusive divide. But in some poetry the language moves beyond that of religious belief, in the ordinary sense, to that of passionate love. William Baldwin has Christ speaking in this language to his 'Spouse', which would, in strict biblical terminology, be the Church, but seems to be the individual believer:

Lo, thou, my Love, art fair;
Myself have made thee so:
Yea, thou art fair indeed,
Wherefore thou shalt not need
In beauty to despair;
For I accept thee so...

The twin poem, to 'Christ, my Beloved', has even stronger overtones of the language of love, indeed, is almost sexual in its intensity:

My Love in me and I in him,
  Conjoined by love, will still abide
    Among the faithful lilies
Till day do break...

The echo of the 'Song of Songs' from the Hebrew scriptures is unmistakeable.

Closer to the language of Christian devotion, but nevertheless mystical in its intensity, is Christina Rossetti's poem, 'After Communion'. Clearly for her receiving communion brought a deep joy and a powerful awareness of Christ's love. But, she wonders, if that is so now, with all the distractions of earth, what will it be like in 'the time of love', the moment of meeting him in eternity?

  Now Thou dost make me lean upon Thy breast:
How will it be with me in time of love?

But not all mystical awareness is expressed in terms of orthodox Christian devotion. For Dylan Thomas, the 'breaking of bread', which draws Christina Rossetti into the arms of Christ, reminds him more of the surging life of nature. The bread and wine are 'born of the sensual root and sap', product of man who 'laid the crops low, broke the grape's joy'. Thomas may have known more about wine than he did about theology, but there is a fascinating glimpse there of the costliness of bread and wine, in ordinary experience, as well as in the sense that Rossetti would have understood it.

Doubt and Faith

Doubt is first cousin to faith, of course, and for many of the poets the two live in creative tension. George Herbert was a man of faith, true, yet –

Love bade me welcome: yet my soul drew back,
    Guiltie of dust and sinne.

John Donne's doubts, too, are not about the truth of the faith, but his own worthiness as a disciple of Christ. He seems to be burdened by the memory of past sins, and perhaps a present reluctance to let go of other affections:

Seale then this bill of my Divorce to All,
On whom those fainter beames of love did falle;
Marry those loves, which in youth scattered bee
On Fame, Wit, Hopes (false mistresses) to thee.

Other poets, especially some of the modern ones, express not so much doubt (in the traditional sense) as misgiving. The Caribbean poet Mervyn Morris offers pictures of two characters from the gospel who preferred compromise to commitment. There is Joseph of Arimathea, the man whose tomb became the burial place of Jesus, a prominent Jewish leader who had presumably remained silent until the execution was over – 'Sometimes, avoiding trouble, we accept defeat' – and the enigmatic figure of Pilate, who declared Jesus innocent as charged, but yet allowed him to go to crucifixion: 'I washed these loving / histrionic hands…'

Or there is John Burnside's Simon of Cyrene, the man who was forced to carry the cross of Jesus to Golgotha, the 'definitive bystander', the very modern man who doesn't like to get involved:

He wasn't meant
    to get involved like this.
Like everyone
    he should be somewhere else.

Alongside doubt and misgiving comes scepticism, which a poet like William Blake employs as crude energy in many of his writings. Blake was a believer, in a deeply mystical sense, but had little time for 'religion' in its organized form. Indeed, he saw its followers as dupes, pursuing an illusion:

We are led to Believe a Lie
When we see not Thro' the Eye…

God in his infinite glory is simply a blinding light to 'poor souls', but, in an intriguing juxtaposition, Christ is there, in 'human form', for those who have eyes to see him:

God Appears & God is Light
To those poor souls who dwell in Night,
But does a Human Form Display
To those who Dwell in Realms of day.

Algernon Charles Swinburne was another poet who found energy in scepticism. His 'Hymn to Proserpine' imagines a Roman reflecting on the consequences of the proclamation in the empire of the Christian faith. It will be the end of laughter, of fun, of sex and passion:

Thou hast conquered, O pale Galilean; the world has grown grey from thy breath...

He admits the 'new Gods' are 'merciful, clothed with pity, the young compassionate Gods', but why must they overthrow everything?

Wilt thou yet take all, Galilean? but these thou shalt not take,
The laurel, the palms and the pæan, the breasts of the nymphs
in the brake...

Much the same feeling is expressed in a poem in the next section, Harold Monro's 'Children of Love', where Cupid meets the young Jesus. It is strange how persistent the idea is that in some deep way Christianity is anti-life, anti-joy and anti-sex. Or perhaps it isn't, when one considers some of the things the Church and its people have said over the centuries.

A great and beautiful part of the human experience of Christ is a longing to discover him or to know him better, and that longing is reflected in many of these poems. Here is John Donne, still wrestling with his guilt as he pens a 'Hymne to God, my God, in my sicknesse':

... As I come
I tune the Instrument here at the dore,
And what I must doe then, thinke now before.

The American, Emily Dickinson, captures the essence of this longing in her lovely poem 'I should have been too glad':

'Tis beggars banquets best define,
'Tis thirsting vitalizes wine.
Faith bleats to understand.

In Evelyn Underhill's poem 'Immanence' the search uncovers the Lord who comes in 'little things', reaching out to the human heart by taking 'Love's highway of humility':

I come in the little things,
Saith the Lord:
My starry wings I do forsake,
Love's highway of humility to take...

– and, having trodden the human path:

I shall achieve my Immemorial Plan,
Pass the low lintel of the human heart.

Oscar Wilde also finds comfort in the humanity of Jesus, writing 'from the shadows' of despair, 'E Tenebris'. For him faith seems to centre on the suffering Christ: 'The wounded hands, the weary human face'.

Patricia St John is not usually counted among the established English poets, but one of her poems, 'The Alchemist', certainly deserves a place in this collection. It addresses the same longing that Dickinson and Wilde expressed, to turn earth's despair and failure into something of ultimate value and worth. Christ 'on our ruins sets a price':

And stooping very low engraves with care
His Name, indelible, upon our dust;
And from the ashes of our self-despair
Kindles a flame of hope and humble trust.

Another woman poet of this century, Kathleen Jamie, draws from her experience in Africa to express a different longing for God, not for herself, but for the people of the villages she came to know and love. She would:

... listen in village lanes
of bones and dung for Jesus' name
among the shouts...

Not every longing is simply to 'know Christ', of course. For the black American poet Countee Cullen it is to relate her own experience of life to one she thinks of as a 'white man':

Wishing He I served were black,
Thinking then it would not lack
Precedent of pain to guide it...

And for R.S. Thomas, the Welsh priest-poet, the longing is for understanding, for answers to torturing questions of faith, longings which are breathed into the still air of a country church:

… There is no other sound
In the darkness but the sound of a man
Breathing, testing his faith
On emptiness, nailing his questions
One by one to an untenanted cross.

Here, and all through the poems in this section, is the Christ of human experience: elusive, haunting, beautiful, and sometimes, it feels, tantalizingly out of reach.

 From: *Troilus and Cressida*

O young fresh folk, whether boy or girl,
In whom love ever grows up with your years
Turn now away from worldly vanity!
And from your heart lift up your young visage
To the very God who after his own image
Made you; and reckon this world's passing hours
Will last no longer than the fading flowers!

And turn your love to Him, who in his love
Upon a cross, our souls to save today,
First died, then rose, and sits in heaven above;
And now will fail no-one, I dare to say,
That will his holy heart upon Him lay!
And since he best to love is, and most meek,
Why should we feigned loves go to seek?

Geoffrey Chaucer (c.1343–1400)

All my Luve, Leave me Not

All my luve, leave me not,
Leave me not, leave me not,
All my luve, leave me not
    Thus mine alone.
With ane burden on my back,
I may not bear it I am sa waik,
Luve, this burden fra me take
    Or ellis I am gone.

With sinnis I am laden sore,
Leave me not, leave me not,
With sinnis I am laden sore
    Leave me not alone.
I pray Thee, Lord, therefore,
Keep not my sinnis in store,
Loose me or I be forlore,
    And hear my moan.

With Thy handis Thou has me wrocht,
Leave me not, leave me not,
With Thy handis Thou has me wrocht,
    Leave me not alone.
I was sold and Thou me bocht,
With Thy blude Thou has me coft,
Now am I hither socht
    To Thee, Lord, alone.

I cry and I call to Thee,
To leave me not, to leave me not,
I cry and I call to Thee
To leave me not alone.
    All they that laden be
Thou biddis come to Thee
Then sall they savit be
    Through Thy mercy alone.

Anonymous (Scottish)

Coft: bought

Christ to his Spouse

Lo, thou, my Love, art fair;
Myself have made thee so:
Yea, thou art fair indeed,
Wherefore thou shalt not need
In beauty to despair;
For I accept thee so,
For fair.

For fair, because thine eyes
Are like the culvers' white,
Whose simpleness in deed
All others do exceed:
Thy judgement wholly lies
In true sense of sprite
Most wise.

William Baldwin (1547–?)

Christ, my Beloved

Christ, my Beloved which still doth feed
Among the flowers, having delight
Among his faithful lilies,
Doth take great care for me indeed,
And I again with all my might
Will do what so his will is.

My Love in me and I in him,
Conjoined by love, will still abide
Among the faithful lilies
Till day do break, and truth do dim
All shadows dark and cause them slide,
According as his will is.

William Baldwin (1547–?)

A Hymne to Christ

At the Author's Last Going into Germany

In what torne ship soever I embarke,
That ship shall be my embleme of thy Arke;
What sea soever swallow mee, that flood
Shall be to mee an embleme of thy blood;
Though thou with clouds of anger do disguise
Thy face, yet through that maske I know those eyes,
    Which, though they turne away sometimes,
        They never will despise.

I sacrifice this Iland unto thee,
And all whom I lov'd there, and who lov'd mee,
When I have put our seas twixt them and mee,
Put thou thy sea betwixt my sinnes and thee.
As the trees sap doth seek the root below
In winter, in my winter now I goe,
    Where none but thee th' Eternall root
        Of true love I may know.

Nor thou nor thy religion dost controule,
The amourousnesse of an harmonious Soule,
But thou would'st have that love thy selfe: As thou
Art jealous Lord, so I am jealous now,
Thou lov'st not, till from loving more, thou free
My soule: Who ever gives, takes libertie,
    O, if thou car'st not whom I love
        Alas, thou lov'st not mee.

Seale then this bill of my Divorce to All,
On whom those fainter beames of love did falle;
Marry those loves, which in youth scattered bee
On Fame, Wit, Hopes (false mistresses) to thee.
Churches are best for Prayer, that have least light.
To see God only, I goe out of sight:
    And to scape stormy dayes, I chuse
        An Everlasting night.

John Donne (1572–1631)

What if this Present were the World's Last Night?

What if this present were the world's last night?
Mark in my heart, O Soul, where thou dost dwell,
The picture of Christ crucified, and tell
Whether that countenance can thee affright.
Tears in his eyes quench the amazing light,
Blood fills his frowns, which from his pierc'd head fell.
And can that tongue adjudge thee unto hell
Which pray'd forgiveness for his foes' fierce spite?
No, no; but as in my idolatry
I said to all my profane mistresses,
'Beauty, of pity, foulness only is
A sign of rigour', so I say to thee:
To wicked spirits are horrid shapes assign'd,
This beauteous form assures a piteous mind.

John Donne (1572–1631)

Hymne to God my God, in my Sicknesse

Since I am comming to that Holy roome,
  Where, with thy Quire of Saints for evermore,
I shall be made thy Musique; As I come
  I tune the Instrument here at the dore,
  And what I must doe then, thinke now before.

Whilst my Physitians by their love are growne
  Cosmographers, and I their Mapp, who lie
Flat on this bed, that by them may be showne
  That this is my South-west discoverie
  Per fretum febris, by these streights to die,

I joy, that in these straits, I see my West:
  For though their currants yeeld return to none,
What shall my West hurt me? As West and East
  In all flat Maps (and I am one) are one,
  So death doth touch the Resurrection.

Is the Pacifique Sea my home? Or are
  The Easterne riches? Is *Jerusalem?*
Anyan, and *Magellan*, and *Gibraltare*,
  All streights, and none but streights, are wayes to them,
  Whether where *Japhet* dwelt, or *Cham*, or *Sem*.

We thinke that *Paradise* and *Calvarie*,
  Christs Crosse, and *Adams* tree, stood in one place;
Looke Lord, and finde both *Adams* met in me;
  As the first *Adams* sweat surrounds my face,
  May the last *Adams* blood my soule embrace.

So, in his purple wrapp'd receive mee Lord,
  By these his thornes give me his other Crowne;
And as to others soules I preach'd thy word,
  Be this my Text, my Sermon to mine owne,
Therfore that he may raise the Lord throws down.

John Donne (1572–1631)

Love

Love bade me welcome: yet my soul drew back,
 Guiltie of dust and sinne.
But quick-ey'd Love, observing me grow slack
 From my first entrance in,
Drew nearer to me, sweetly questioning,
 If I lack'd any thing.

A guest, I answer'd, worthy to be here:
 Love said, You shall be he.
I the unkinde, ungratefull? Ah my deare,
 I cannot look on thee.
Love took my hand, and smiling did reply,
 Who made the eyes but I?

Truth Lord, but I have marr'd them: let my shame
 Go where it doth deserve.
And know you not, sayes Love, who bore the blame?
 My deare, then I will serve.
You must sit downe, sayes Love, and taste my meat:
 So I did sit and eat.

George Herbert (1593–1633)

Christmas

All after pleasures as I rid one day,
    My horse and I, both tir'd, bodie and minde,
    With full crie of affections, quite astray,
I took up in the next inne I could finde.
There when I came, whom found I but my deare,
    My dearest Lord, expecting till the grief
    Of pleasures brought me to him, readie there
To be all passengers most sweet relief?
O Thou, whose glorious, yet contracted light,
    Wrapt in nights mantle, stole into a manger;
    Since my dark soul and brutish is thy right,
To Man of all beasts be not thou a stranger:
    Furnish & deck my soul, that thou mayst have
    A better lodging then a rack or grave.

The shepherds sing; and shall I silent be?
    My God, no hymne for thee?
My soul's a shepherd too; a flock it feeds
    Of thoughts, and words, and deeds.
The pasture is thy word: the streams, thy grace
    Enriching all the place.
Shepherd and flock shall sing, and all my powers
    Out-sing the day-light houres.
Then we will chide the sunne for letting night
    Take up his place and right:
We sing one common Lord; wherefore he should
    Himself the candle hold.
I will go searching, till I finde a sunne
    Shall stay, till we have done;
A willing shiner, that shall shine as gladly,
    As frost-nipt sunnes look sadly.
Then we will sing, and shine all our own day,
    And one another pay:
His beams shall cheer my breast, and both so twine,
Till ev'n his beams sing, and my musick shine.

George Herbert (1593–1633)

Aaron

Holinesse on the head,
Light and perfections on the breast,
Harmonious bells below, raising the dead
To leade them unto life and rest:
Thus are true Aarons drest.

Profanenesse in my head,
Defects and darknesse in my breast,
A noise of passions ringing me for dead
Unto a place where is no rest:
Poore priest thus am I drest.

Onely another head
I have, another heart and breast,
Another musick, making live not dead,
Without whom I could have no rest:
In him I am well drest.

Christ is my onely head,
My alone onely heart and breast,
My onely musick, striking me ev'n dead;
That to the old man I may rest,
And be in him new drest.

So holy in my head,
Perfect and light in my deare breast,
My doctrine tun'd by Christ, (who is not dead,
But lives in me while I do rest)
Come people; Aaron's drest.

George Herbert (1593–1633)

Aaron: the High Priest of Israel, who wore the insignia 'Holiness to the Lord' on his vestment

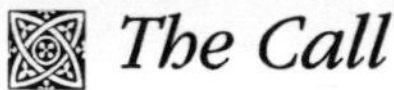 The Call

Come, my Way, my Truth, my Life:
Such a Way, as gives us breath:
Such a Truth, as ends all strife:
Such a Life, as killeth death.

Come, my Light, my Feast, my Strength:
Such a Light, as shows a feast:
Such a Feast, as mends in length:
Such a Strength, as makes his guest.

Come, my Joy, my Love, my Heart:
Such a Joy, as none can move:
Such a Love, as none can part:
Such a Heart, as joys in love.

George Herbert (1593–1633)

A Dialogue

Man. Sweetest Saviour, if my soul
Were but worth the having,
Quickly should I then control
Any thought of waving.
But when all my care and pains
Cannot give the name of gains
To Thy wretch so full of stains,
What delight or hope remains?

Saviour. What, child, is the balance thine,
Thine the poise and measure?
If I say, 'Thou shalt be Mine,'
Finger not My treasure.
What the gains in having thee
Do amount to, only He
Who for man was sold can see
That transferr'd th' accounts to Me.

Man. But as I can see no merit
Leading to this favour,
So the way to fit me for it
Is beyond my savour.
As the reason, then, is Thine,
So the way is none of mine;
I disclaim the whole design;
Sin disclaims and I resign.

Saviour. That is all: if that I could
Get without repining;
And My clay, My creature, would
Follow My resigning;
That as I did freely part
With My glory and desert,
Left all joys to feel all smart –

Man. Ah, no more! Thou break'st my heart!

George Herbert (1593–1633)

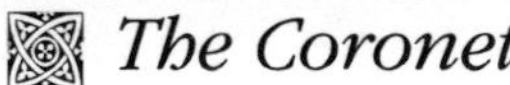

The Coronet

When for the Thorns with which I long, too long,
    With many a piercing wound
    My Saviour's head have crown'd,
I seek with Garlands to redress that Wrong,
    Through every Garden, every Mead
I gather flow'rs (my fruits are only flow'rs)
    Dismantling all the fragrant Towers
That once adorn'd my Shepherdess's head.
And now when I have summ'd up all my store,
    Thinking (so I my self deceive)
    So rich a Chaplet thence to weave
As never yet the king of Glory wore,
    Alas I find the Serpent old
    That, twining in his speckled breast,
    About the flow'rs disguis'd does fold,
    With wreaths of Fame and Interest.
Ah, foolish Man, that would'st debase with them
And mortal Glory, Heaven's Diadem!
But thou who only could'st the Serpent tame,
Either his slipp'ry knots at once untie,
And disintangle all his winding Snare;
Or shatter too with him my curious frame
And let these wither, so that he may die,
Though set with Skill and chosen out with Care;
That they, while Thou on both their Spoils dost tread,
May crown thy Feet, that could not crown thy Head.

Andrew Marvell (1621–78)

Christian's Song

From: The Pilgrim's Progress

Thus far I did come laden with my sin;
Nor could aught ease the grief that I was in
Till I came hither; What a place is this:
Must here be the beginning of my bliss?
Must here the burden fall from off my back?
Must here the strings that bound it to me crack?
Blest cross! blest sepulchre! blest rather be
The man that there was put to shame for me!

John Bunyan (1628–88)

The Divine Image

To Mercy, Pity, Peace, and Love
All pray in their distress;
And to these virtues of delight
Return their thankfulness.

For Mercy, Pity, Peace, and Love
Is God, our father dear,
And Mercy, Pity, Peace, and Love
Is Man, his child and care.

For Mercy has a human heart,
Pity a human face,
And Love, the human form divine,
And Peace, the human dress.

Then every man, of every clime,
That prays in his distress,
Prays to the human form divine,
Love, Mercy, Pity, Peace.

And all must love the human form,
In heathen, turk, or jew;
Where Mercy, Love, & Pity dwell
There God is dwelling too.

William Blake (1757–1827)

From: Auguries of Innocence

To see a World in a Grain of Sand
And a Heaven in a Wild Flower,
Hold Infinity in the palm of your hand
And Eternity in an hour...

Every Night & every Morn
Some to Misery are Born.
Every Morn & every Night
Some are Born to sweet delight.
Some are Born to sweet delight,
Some are Born to Endless Night.
We are led to Believe a Lie
When we see not Thro' the Eye
Which was Born in a Night to perish in a Night
When the Soul Slept in Beams of Light.
God Appears & God is Light
To those poor Souls who dwell in Night,
But does a Human Form Display
To those who Dwell in Realms of day.

William Blake (1757–1827)

On Another's Sorrow

Can I see another's woe,
And not be in sorrow too?
Can I see another's grief,
And not seek for kind relief?

Can I see a falling tear,
And not feel my sorrow's share?
Can a father see his child
Weep, nor be with sorrow fill'd?

Can a mother sit and hear
An infant groan an infant fear?
No, no! never can it be!
Never, never can it be!

And can he who smiles on all
Hear the wren with sorrows small,
Hear the small bird's grief & care,
Hear the woes that infants bear,

And not sit beside the nest,
Pouring pity in their breast;
And not sit the cradle near,
Weeping tear on infant's tear;

And not sit both night & day,
Wiping all our tears away?
O, no! never can it be!
Never, never can it be!

He doth give his joy to all;
He becomes an infant small;
He becomes a man of woe;
He doth feel the sorrow too.

Think not thou canst sigh a sigh
And thy maker is not by;
Think not thou canst weep a tear
And thy maker is not near.

O! he gives to us his joy
That our grief he may destroy;
Till our grief is fled & gone
He doth sit by us and moan.

William Blake (1757–1827)

The Three Enemies

The Flesh

'Sweet, thou art pale.'
            'More pale to see,
Christ hung upon the cruel tree
And hung upon the cruel tree
And bore His Father's wrath for me.'

'Sweet, thou art sad.'
            'Beneath a rod
More heavy, Christ for my sake trod
The winepress of the wrath of God.'

'Sweet, thou art weary.'
            'Not so Christ;
Whose mighty love of me sufficed
For Strength, Salvation, Eucharist.'

'Sweet, thou art footsore.'
            'If I bleed,
His feet have bled; yea in my need
His Heart once bled for mine indeed.'

The World

'Sweet, thou art young.'
            'So He was young
Who for my sake in silence hung
Upon the Cross with Passion wrung.'

'Look, thou art fair.'
            'He was more fair
Than men, who deigned for me to wear
A visage marred beyond compare.'

'And thou hast riches.'
          'Daily bread:
All else is His: Who, living, dead,
For me lacked where to lay His Head.'

'And life is sweet.'
          'It was not so
To Him, Whose Cup did overflow
With mine unutterable woe.'

The Devil

'Thou drinkest deep.'
          'When Christ would sup
He drained the dregs from out my cup:
So how should I be lifted up?'

'Thou shalt win Glory.'
          'In the skies,
Lord Jesus, cover up mine eyes
Lest they should look on vanities.'

'Thou shalt have Knowledge.'
          'Helpless dust!
In thee, O Lord, I put my trust:
Answer Thou for me, Wise and Just.'

'And Might.' –
          'Get thee behind me. Lord,
Who hast redeemed and not abhorred
My soul, oh keep it by Thy Word.'

Christina Rossetti (1830–94)

A Bruised Reed Shall He not Break

I will accept thy will to do and be,
   Thy hatred and intolerance of sin,
   Thy will at least to love, that burns within
      And thirsteth after Me:
So will I render fruitful, blessing still,
   The germs and small beginnings in thy heart,
   Because thy will cleaves to the better part –
      Alas, I cannot will.

Dost not thou will, poor soul? Yet I receive
   The inner unseen longings of the soul,
   I guide them turning towards Me; I control
      And charm hearts till they grieve;
If thou desire, it yet shall come to pass,
   Though thou but wish indeed to choose My love;
   For I have power in earth and heaven above –
      I cannot wish, alas!

What, neither choose nor wish to choose? and yet
   I still must strive to win thee and constrain:
   For thee I hung upon the cross in pain,
      How then can I forget?
If thou as yet dost neither love, nor hate,
   Nor choose, nor wish – resign thyself, be still
   Till I infuse love, hatred, longing, will –
      I do not deprecate.

Christina Rossetti (1830–94)

After Communion

Why should I call Thee Lord, Who art my God?
Why should I call Thee Friend, who art my Love?
Or King, Who art my very Spouse above?
Or call Thy Sceptre on my heart Thy rod?
Lo, now Thy banner over me is love,
All heaven flies open to me at Thy nod:
For Thou hast lit Thy flame in me a clod,
Made me a nest for dwelling of Thy Dove.
What wilt Thou call me in our home above,
Who now hast called me friend? how will it be
When Thou for good wine settest forth the best?
Now Thou dost bid me come and sup with Thee,
Now Thou dost make me lean upon Thy breast:
How will it be with me in time of love?

Christina Rossetti (1830–94)

The Love of Christ which Passeth Knowledge

I bore with thee long weary days and nights,
    Through many pangs of heart, through many tears;
I bore with thee, thy hardness, coldness, slights,
    For three-and-thirty years.

Who else had dared for thee what I have dared?
    I plunged the depth most deep from bliss above;
I not My flesh, I not My spirit spared:
    Give thou Me love for love.

For thee I thirsted in the daily drouth,
    For thee I trembled in the nightly frost:
Much sweeter thou than honey to My mouth:
    Why wilt thou still be lost?

I bore thee on My shoulders and rejoiced:
    Men only marked upon My shoulders borne
The branding cross; and shouted hungry-voiced,
    Or wagged their heads in scorn.

Thee did nails grave upon My hands, thy name
    Did thorns for frontlets stamp between Mine eyes:
I, Holy One, put on thy guilt and shame;
    I, God, Priest, Sacrifice.

A thief upon My right hand and My left;
    Six hours alone, athirst, in misery:
At length in death one smote My heart and cleft
    A hiding-place for thee.

Nailed to the racking cross, than bed of down
    More dear, whereon to stretch Myself and sleep:
So did I win a kingdom – share My crown;
    A harvest – come and reap.

Christina Rossetti (1830–94)

I Should Have Been too Glad

I should have been too glad, I see,
Too lifted for the scant degree
Of life's penurious round;
My little circuit would have shamed
This new circumference, have blamed
The homelier time behind.

I should have been too saved, I see,
Too rescued; fear too dim to me
That I could spell the prayer
I knew so perfect yesterday,
That scalding one, 'Sabachthani',
Recited fluent here.

Earth would have been too much, I see,
And Heaven not enough for me.
I should have had the joy
Without the fear to justify,
The palm without the Calvary.
So, Saviour, crucify.

Defeat whets victory, they say.
The reefs in old Gethsemane
Endear the shore beyond.
'Tis beggars banquets best define,
'Tis thirsting vitalizes wine.
Faith bleats to understand.

Emily Dickinson (1830–86)

Hymn to Proserpine

After the Proclamation in Rome of the Christian Faith
Vicisti, Galilææ

I have lived long enough, having seen one thing, that love hath an end;
Goddess and maiden and queen, be near me now and befriend.
Thou art more than the day or the morrow, the seasons that laugh or that weep;
For these give joy and sorrow; but thou, Proserpina, sleep.
Sweet is the treading of wine, and sweet the feet of the dove;
But a goodlier gift is thine than foam of the grapes or love.
Yea, is not even Apollo, with hair and harpstring of gold,
A bitter God to follow, a beautiful God to behold?
I am sick of singing: the bays burn deep and chafe: I am fain
To rest a little from praise and the grievous pleasure and pain.
For the Gods we know not of, who give us our daily breath,
We know they are cruel as love or life, and lovely as death.
O Gods dethroned and deceased, cast forth, wiped out in a day!
From your wrath is the world released, redeemed from your chains, men say.
New Gods are crowned in the city; their flowers have broken your rods;
They are merciful, clothed with pity, the young compassionate Gods.
But for me their new device is barren, the days are bare;
Things long past over suffice, and men forgotten that were.
Time and the Gods are at strife; ye dwell in the midst thereof,
Draining a little life from the barren breasts of love.
I say to you, cease, take rest; yea, I say to you all, be at peace,
Till the bitter milk of her breast and the barren bosom shall cease,
Wilt thou yet take all, Galilean? but these thou shalt not take,
The laurel, the palms and the pæan, the breasts of the nymphs in the brake;
Breasts more soft than a dove's, that tremble with tenderer breath;
And all the wings of the Loves, and all the joy before death;
All the feet of the hours that sound as a single lyre,
Dropped and deep in the flowers, with strings that flicker like fire.
More than these wilt thou give, things fairer than all these things?
Nay, for a little we live, and life hath mutable wings.
A little while and we die; shall life not thrive as it may?
For no man under the sky lives twice, outliving his day.

And grief is a grievous thing, and a man hath enough of his tears:
Why should he labour, and bring fresh grief to blacken his years?
Thou hast conquered, O pale Galilean; the world has grown grey
from thy breath;
We have drunken of things Lethean, and fed on the fullness of
death.
Laurel is green for a season, and love is sweet for a day;
But love grows bitter with treason, and laurel outlives not May.
Sleep, shall we sleep after all? for the world is not sweet in the end;
For the old faiths loosen and fall, the new years ruin and rend.
Fate is a sea without shore, and the soul is a rock that abides;
But her ears are vexed with the roar and her face with the foam of
the tides.
O lips that the live blood faints in, the leavings of racks and rods!
O ghastly glories of saints, dead limbs of gibbeted Gods!
Though all men abase them before you in spirit, and all knees
bend,
I kneel not neither adore you, but standing, look to the end.
All delicate days and pleasant, all spirits and sorrows are cast
Far out with the foam of the present that sweeps to the surf of the
past:
Where beyond the extreme sea-wall, and between the remote sea-
gates,
Waste water washes, and tall ships founder, and deep death waits:
Where, mighty with deepening sides, clad about with the seas as
with wings,
And impelled of invisible tides, and fulfilled of unspeakable things,
White-eyed and poisonous-finned, shark-toothed and serpentine-
curled,
Rolls, under the whitening wind of the future, the wave of the
world.
The depths stand naked in sunder behind it, the storms flee away;
In the hollow before it the thunder is taken and snared as a prey;
In its sides is the north-wind bound; and its salt is of all men's tears;
With light of ruin, and sound of changes, and pulse of years:
With travail of day after day, and with trouble of hour upon hour;
And bitter as blood is the spray; and the crests are as fangs that
devour:
And its vapour and storm of its steam as the sighing of spirits to be;
And its noise as the noise in a dream; and its depth as the roots of
the sea:
And the height of its heads as the height of the utmost stars of the
air;

And the ends of the earth at the might thereof tremble, and time is made bare.
Will ye bridle the deep sea with reins, will ye chasten the high sea with rods?
Will ye take her to chain her with chains, who is older than all ye Gods?
Sent down unto us that besought her, and earth grew sweet with her name.
For thine came weeping, a slave among slaves, and rejected; but she
Came flushed from the full-flushed wave, and imperial, her foot on the sea.
And the wonderful waters knew her, the winds and the viewless ways,
And the roses grew rosier, and bluer the sea-blue stream of the bays.
Ye are fallen, our lords, by what token? we wist that ye should not fall.
Ye were all so fair that are broken; and one more fair than ye all.
But I turn to her still, having seen she shall surely abide in the end;
Goddess and maiden and queen, be near me now and befriend.
O daughter of earth, of my mother, her crown and blossom of birth,
I am also, I also, thy brother; I go as I came unto earth.
In the night where thine eyes are as moons are in heaven, the night where thou art,
Where the silence is more than all tunes, where sleep overflows from the heart,
Where the poppies are sweet as the rose in our world, and the red rose is white,
And the wind falls faint as it blows with the fume of the flowers of the night,
And the murmur of spirits that sleep in the shadow of Gods from afar
Grows dim in thine ears and deep as the deep dim soul of a star,
And ye as a wind shall go by, as a fire shall ye pass and be past;
Ye are Gods, and behold, ye shall die, and the waves be upon you at last.
In the darkness of time, in the deeps of the years, in the changes of things,
Ye shall sleep as a slain man sleeps, and the world shall forget you for kings.
Though the feet of thine high priests tread where thy lords and our forefathers trod,

Though these that were Gods are dead, and thou being dead art a God,
Though before thee the throned Cytherean be fallen, and hidden her head,
Yet thy kingdom shall pass, Galilean, thy dead shall go down to thee dead.
Of the maiden thy mother men sing as a goddess with grace clad around;
Thou art throned where another was king; where another was queen she is crowned.
Yea, once we had sight of another: but now she is queen, say these.
Not as thine, not as thine was our mother, a blossom of flowering seas,
Clothed round with the world's desire as with raiment, and fair as the foam,
And fleeter than kindled fire, and a goddess, and mother of Rome.
For thine came pale and a maiden, and sister to sorrow; but ours,
Her deep hair heavily laden with odour and colour of flowers,
White rose of the rose-white water, a silver splendour, a flame,
In the sweet low light of thy face, under heavens untrod by the sun,
Let my soul with their souls find place, and forget what is done and undone.
Thou art more than the Gods who number the days of our temporal breath;
For these give labour and slumber; but thou, Proserpina, death.
Therefore now at thy feet I abide for a season in silence. I know
I shall die as my fathers died, and sleep as they sleep; even so.
For the glass of the years is brittle wherein we gaze for a span;
A little soul for a little bears up this corpse which is man.
So long I endure, no longer; and laugh not again, neither weep.
For there is no God found stronger than death; and death is a sleep.

Algernon Charles Swinburne (1837–1909)

Hurrahing in Harvest

Summer ends now; now, barbarous in beauty, the stooks rise
Around; up above, what wind-walks! what lovely behaviour
Of silk-sack clouds! has wilder, wilful-wavier
Meal-drift moulded ever and melted across skies?

I walk, I lift up, I lift up heart, eyes,
Down all that glory in the heavens to glean our Saviour;
And, éyes, héart, what looks, what lips yet gave you a
Rapturous love's greeting of realer, of rounder replies?

And the azurous hung hills are his world-wielding shoulder
Majestic – as a stallion stalwart, very-violet-sweet! –
These things, these things were here and but the beholder
Wanting; which two when they once meet,
The heart rears wings bold and bolder
And hurls for him, O half hurls earth for him off under his feet.

Gerard Manley Hopkins (1844–89)

S. Thomae Aquinatis

Rhythmus ad SS. Sacramentum
'Adoro te supplex, latens deitas'

Godhead here in hiding, whom I do adore
Masked by these bare shadows, shape and nothing more,
See, Lord, at thy service low lies here a heart
Lost, all lost in wonder at the God thou art.

Seeing, touching, tasting are in thee deceived;
How says trusty hearing? that shall be believed;
What God's Son has told me, take for truth I do;
Truth himself speaks truly or there's nothing true.

On the cross thy godhead made no sign to men;
Here thy very manhood steals from human ken:
Both are my confession, both are my belief,
And I pray the prayer of the dying thief.

I am not like Thomas, wounds I cannot see,
But can plainly call thee Lord and God as he:
This faith each day deeper be my holding of,
Daily make me harder hope and dearer love.

O thou our reminder of Christ crucified,
Living Bread the life of us for whom he died,
Lend this life to me then: feed and feast my mind,
There be thou the sweetness man was meant to find.

Bring the tender tale true of the Pelican;
Bathe me, Jesu Lord, in what thy bosom ran –
Blood that but one drop of has the world to win
All the world forgiveness of its world of sin.

Jesu whom I look at shrouded here below,
I beseech thee send me what I thirst for so,
Some day to gaze on thee face to face in light
And be blest for ever with thy glory's sight.

Gerard Manley Hopkins (1844–89)

 *As Kingfishers Catch Fire*

As kingfishers catch fire, dragonflies draw flame;
   As tumbled over rim in roundy wells
   Stones ring; like each tucked string tells, each hung bell's
Bow swung finds tongue to fling out broad its name;
Each mortal thing does one thing and the same:
   Deals out that being indoors each one dwells;
   Selves – goes itself; *myself* it speaks and spells,
Crying *What I do is me: for that I came*.

I say more: the just man justices;
   Keeps gráce: thát keeps all his goings graces;
Acts in God's eye what in God's eye he is –
   Chríst. For Christ plays in ten thousand places,
Lovely in limbs, and lovely in eyes not his
   To the Father through the features of men's faces.

Gerard Manley Hopkins (1844–89)

 *E Tenebris*

Come down, O Christ, and help me! reach thy hand,
   For I am drowning in a stormier sea
   Than Simon on thy lake of Galilee:
The wine of life is spilt upon the sand,
My heart is as some famine-murdered land
   Whence all good things have perished utterly
   And well I know my soul in Hell must lie
If I this night before God's throne should stand.
'He sleeps perchance, or rideth to the chase,
   Like Baal, when his prophets howled that name
   From morn to noon on Carmel's smitten height.'
Nay, peace, I shall behold, before the night,
   The feet of brass, the robe more white than flame,
The wounded hands, the weary human face.

Oscar Wilde (1854–1900)

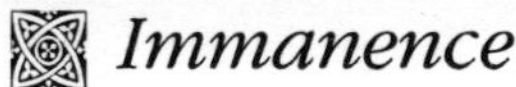

Immanence

I come in the little things,
Saith the Lord:
Not borne on morning wings
Of majesty, but I have set My Feet
Amidst the delicate and bladed wheat
That springs triumphant in the furrowed sod.
There do I dwell, in weakness and in power,
Not broken or divided, saith our God!
In your strait garden plot I come to:
About your porch My Vine
Meek, fruitful, doth entwine;
Waits, at the threshold, Love's appointed time.

I come in the little things,
Saith the Lord:
Yea! on the glancing wings
Of eager birds, the softly pattering feet
Of furred and gentle beasts, I come to meet
Your hard and wayward heart. In brown bright eyes
That peep from out the brake, I stand confest.
On every nest
Where feathery Patience is content to brood
And leaves her pleasure for the high emprize
Of motherhood –
There doth My Godhead rest.

I come in the little things,
Saith the Lord:
My starry wings I do forsake,
Love's highway of humility to take:
Meekly I fit your stature to your need.
In beggar's part
About your gates I shall not cease to plead –
As man, to speak with man –
Till by such art
I shall achieve my Immemorial Plan,
Pass the low lintel of the human heart.

Evelyn Underhill (1875–1941)

From: Heritage

Quaint, outlandish heathen gods
Black men fashion out of rods,
Clay, and brittle bits of stone,
In a likeness like their own,
My conversion came high-priced;
I belong to Jesus Christ,
Preacher of humility;
Heathen gods are naught to me.

Father, Son, and Holy Ghost,
So I make an idle boast;
Jesus of the twice-turned cheek,
Lamb of God, although I speak
With my mouth thus, in my heart
Do I play a double part.
Ever at Thy glowing altar
Must my heart grow sick and falter,
Wishing He I served were black,
Thinking then it would not lack
Precedent of pain to guide it,
Let who would or might deride it;
Surely then this flesh would know
Yours had borne a kindred woe,
Lord, I fashion dark gods, too,
Daring even to give You,
Dark despairing features where,
Crowned with dark rebellious hair.
Patience wavers just so much as
Mortal grief compels, while touches
Quick and hot, of anger, rise
To smitten cheek and weary eyes.
Lord, forgive me if my need
Sometimes shapes a human creed.

All day long and all night through,
One thing only must I do:
Quench my pride and cool my blood,
Lest I perish in the flood.
Lest a hidden ember set
Timber that I thought was wet
Burning like the dryest flax,
Melting like the merest wax,
Lest the grave restore its dead.
Nor yet has my heart or head
In the least way realized
They and I are civilized.

Countee Cullen (1903–46)

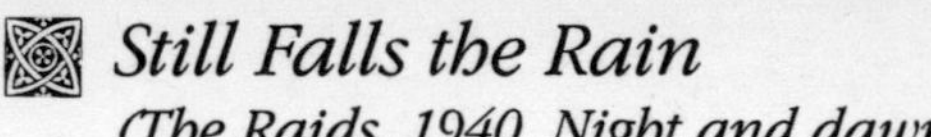

Still Falls the Rain
(The Raids, 1940. Night and dawn.)

Still falls the Rain –
Dark as the world of man, black as our loss –
Blind as the nineteen hundred and forty nails
Upon the Cross.

Still falls the Rain
With a sound like the pulse of the heart that is changed to the
hammer-beat
In the Potter's Field, and the sound of the impious feet

On the Tomb:
Still falls the Rain
In the Field of Blood where the small hopes breed and the
human brain
Nurtures its greed, that worm with the brow of Cain.

Still falls the Rain
At the feet of the Starved Man hung upon the Cross.
Christ that each day, each night, nails there,
have mercy on us –
On Dives and on Lazarus:
Under the Rain the sore and the gold are as one.

Still falls the Rain –
still falls the blood from the Starved Man's wounded Side:
He bears in his Heart all wounds – those of the light
that died,
The last faint spark
In the self-murdered heart, the wounds of the sad
uncomprehending dark,
The wounds of the baited bear –
The blind and weeping bear whom the keepers beat
On his helpless flesh... the tears of the hunted hare.

Still falls the Rain –
Then – O Ile leape up to my God: who pulles me doune –
See, see where Christ's blood streames in the firmament:
It flows from the Brow we nailed upon the tree
Deep to the dying, to the thirsting heart
That holds the fires of the world – dark-smirched with pain
As Caesar's laurel crown.

Then sounds the voice of One who like the heart of man
Was once a child who among beasts has lain –
'Still do I love, still shed my innocent light, my Blood, for thee.'

Edith Sitwell (1887–1964)

This Bread I Break

This bread I break was once the oat,
This wine upon a foreign tree
Plunged in its fruit;
Man in the day or wind at night
Laid the crops low, broke the grape's joy.

Once in this wine the summer blood
Knocked in the flesh that decked the vine,
Once in this bread
The oat was merry in the wind;
Man broke the sun, pulled the wind down.

This flesh you break, this blood you let
Make desolation in the vein,
Were oat and grape
Born of the sensual root and sap;
My wine you drink, my bread you snap.

Dylan Thomas (1914–53)

Twelfth Night

No night could be darker than this night,
no cold so cold,
as the blood snaps like a wire,
and the heart's sap stills,
and the year seems defeated.

O never again, it seems, can green things run,
or sky birds fly,
or the grass exhale its humming breath
powdered with pimpernels,
from this dark lung of winter.

Yet here are lessons for the final mile
of pilgrim kings;
the mile still left when all have reached
their tether's end: that mile
where the Child lies hid.

For see, beneath the hand, the earth already
warms and glows;
for men with shepherd's eyes there are
signs in the dark, the turning stars,
the lamb's returning time.

Out of this utter death he's born again,
his birth our saviour;
from terror's equinox he climbs and grows,
drawing his finger's light across our blood
the son of heaven, and the son of God.

Laurie Lee (1914–)

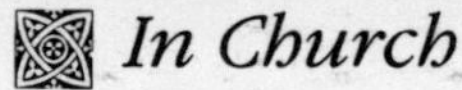

In Church

Often I try
To analyse the quality
Of its silences. Is this where God hides
From my searching? I have stopped to listen,
After the few people have gone,
To the air recomposing itself
For vigil. It has waited like this
Since the stones grouped themselves about it.
These are the hard ribs
Of a body that our prayers have failed
To animate. Shadows advance
From their corners to take possession
Of places that light held
For an hour. The bats resume
Their business. The uneasiness of the pews
Ceases. There is no other sound
In the darkness but the sound of a man
Breathing, testing his faith
On emptiness, nailing his questions
One by one to an untenanted cross.

R.S. Thomas (1913–)

In a Country Church

To one kneeling down no word came,
Only the wind's song, saddening the lips
Of the grave saints, rigid in glass;
Or the dry whisper of unseen wings,
Bats not angels, in the high roof.

Was he balked by silence? He kneeled long,
And saw love in a dark crown
Of thorns blazing, and a winter tree
Golden with fruit of a man's body.

R.S. Thomas (1913–)

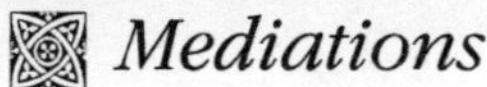

Mediations

And to one God says: Come
to me by numbers and
figures; see my beauty
in the angles between
stars, in the equations
of my kingdom. Bring
your lenses to the worship
of my dimensions: far
out and far in, there
is always more of me
in proportion. And to another:
I am the bush burning
at the centre of
your existence; you must put
your knowledge off and come
to me with your mind
bare. And to this one
he says: Because of
your high stomach, the bleakness
of your emotions, I
will come to you in the simplest
things, in the body
of a man hung on a tall
tree you have converted to
timber and you shall not know me.

R.S. Thomas (1913–)

The Alchemist

My Master an elixir hath that turns
All base and worthless substances to gold.
From rubble stones He fashions palaces
Most beautiful and stately to behold.
He garners with a craftsman's skilful care
All that we break, and weeping cast away.
His eyes see uncut opals in the rock
And shapely vessels in our trampled clay.
The sum of life's lost opportunities,
The broken friendships, and the wasted years,
These are His raw materials; His hands
Rest on the fragments, weld them with His tears.

A patient Alchemist! – He bides His time
Broods while the south winds breathe, the North winds blow,
And weary self, at enmity with self,
Works out its own destruction, bitter slow.
Then when our dreams have dwindled into smoke
Our gallant highways petered out in mire,
Our airy castles crumbled into dust,
Leaving us stripped of all save fierce desire,
He comes, with feet deliberate and slow,
Who counts a contrite heart His sacrifice.
(No other bidders rise to stake their claims,
He only on our ruins sets a price.)
And stooping very low engraves with care
His Name, indelible, upon our dust;
And from the ashes of our self-despair
Kindles a flame of hope and humble trust.
He seeks no second site on which to build,
But on the old foundation, stone by stone,
Cementing sad experience with grace,
Fashions a stronger temple of His own.

Patricia St John (1921–)

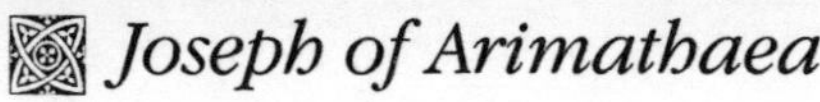

Joseph of Arimathaea

Sometimes, avoiding trouble, we accept defeat.
(Painful sometimes, being discreet.)

Soon Sabbath now. The corpse of Christ
ought to come down by then.
Which means pulling strings again.
I think I'll bury him where I
had planned to have my own bones lie.

Thank God, there's something I can do.
Forgive me, Lord, for not proclaiming you.

Mervyn Morris (1937–)

Pilate

And then I tried to pass the buck;
but Herod, with astute aplomb,
politely, sent him back.

I tried to move the people
to accept he might be freed
this feast of The Passover.
'Kill him! Kill him! Nail him
to the cross!' They clamoured for
Barabbas, insurrectionist, a bandit
who's attacked imperial rule.
'Try Jesus for yourselves,' I told the mob;
'You judge him by your law.'
'Kill him,' they hollered louder,
'Nail him to the cross!'
Then slimy priests, those holy rogues
of politics, began to turn the screws:
'You must not fail to sentence Christ,
soi-disant King of Jews.
Your masters wouldn't like it much
if we should let them know
we caught a man supplanting Rome
and you have let him go.'

My basic job is keeping peace
and reverence for Rome. The man
was bad for both. I had to yield.
'I find no fault in him,' I cried,
and ordered water brought;
and, public gesture of defeat
(sound politics, I thought),
I washed these loving
histrionic hands.

The crowd surprised me, seized
the guilt of their demands.

You know
I am not weak. I could, I would
stand up for Jesus if I thought
that were the thing to do. Now
he is dead. He didn't seem to care,
so why should you? How is your head,
my sweet?

Mervyn Morris (1937–)

Ride upon the Death Chariot

They rode upon
the death chariot
to their Golgotha –
three vagrants
whose papers to be in Caesar's empire
were not in order.

The sun
shrivelled their bodies
in the mobile tomb
as airtight as canned fish.

We're hot!
We're thirsty!
We're hungry!

The centurion
touched their tongues
with the tip
of a lance
dipped in apathy:

'Don't cry to me
but to Caesar who
crucifies you.'

A woman came
to wipe their faces.
She carried a dishcloth
full of bread and tea.

We're dying!

The centurion
washed his hands.

Oswald Mtshali (1940–)

Simon of Cyrene

Here's the definitive
bystander:

trapped in the smell of wood and a scrawl
of dust
he enters what will pass
for history.

Taking the cross from the convict's
birdlike hands

he thinks of his children,
his wife
in her garden of vines,

then shoulders the weight.

He wasn't meant
to get involved in this.

Like everyone
he should be somewhere else.

John Burnside (1955–)

Outreach

With a stick in the hot dust
I draw a tenement, a plane, a church:
my country we have no
family fields, In a smoke-choked hut
where a barren wife gave birth
they pat the sackcloth, *sit*!
while hens peck around the sleeping kids
and someone coughs, coughs. *What your family?*

Hunkered in the mean shade
of our compound walls: *Your tits*
not big! Our yard grows
nothing, their constant feet.
At noon, the murderous heat,
I clang the gate: *come back tomorrow*.
Perhaps in my heart of hearts
I lack compassion. I lie.

hot nights on a straight bed,
watch crowded stars through mosquito mesh
and talk to Jesus. Moonlight strikes
our metal gate like a silent gong.
Sometimes I wake
to a dog's yelp, a screech of owl,
sometimes, a wide-eyed girl
hugely wrapped in shawls. *What your husband?*

I walk a fine line with the headman,
write home: *One day I'll build a church*;
because I believe in these Lazarus' huts
are secret believers;
and listen in village lanes
of bones and dung for Jesus' name
among the shouts, the bleating goats,
the bursts of dirty laughter.

Kathleen Jamie (1962–)

s i x

The Mystery of His Meaning

'The Uncontrollable Mystery'

On one occasion, eighteen months or so into his public ministry, Jesus asked his disciples two vital questions. The first was, 'Who do people say that I am?' The second, even more searching, was, 'But who do *you* say that I am?' To the first question they replied 'John the Baptist, Elijah, or one of the other prophets.' To the second, they replied, through their spokesman, Peter, 'You are the Messiah of God.' From then on, the style of Jesus' ministry changed radically, as he prepared his followers for the inevitable showdown with the religious authorities which culminated in his death.

The interesting thing is that it was the question of his *identity*, of who he is, of his relationship to God, that was the turning point. Indeed, the main 'plot' of the gospels is this question of the true identity of Jesus. Mark depicts it as a kind of secret, which is only to be unveiled at the right moment. That Jesus was unusual, special, unique even, was widely accepted. But the mystery was in the meaning: what did the presence of this 'special' man mean? In what way did he relate to God? What did it mean to say that he was the 'Son of God'? And if he was in some sense of the word 'divine', as his followers began to appreciate after the resurrection, then could he really be described as a human being at all? These were the questions that concerned the Church in its early centuries, and their attempts to define them into comprehensible beliefs led to endless argument, dispute – and even bloodshed.

So the question of the 'meaning' of Jesus was always, and is always, absolutely central to our understanding of him. At one level he lived and acted and spoke like a Jewish rabbi, or like one of the more charismatic prophets of Israel: human, but immensely gifted by God. Yet at another level, according to the gospels, he acted like God himself – forgiving sins, healing the sick, raising the dead, yes, and even daring to re-interpret the very law of God. He called himself, enigmatically, the 'Son of Man', choosing a title found in the Hebrew prophets to describe a special agent or emissary of God, but used in the language of his day to mean something like 'True Human', 'Real Man'. But he did not reject the title 'Son of God' when others applied it to him, while leaving open the way in which it was to be understood.

So there was and is something of a mystery about Jesus – a mystery only resolved by faith. Those who have believed in him down the centuries have not found it difficult to accept the orthodox Christian view that Jesus is both human and divine, sharing fully in both natures. But in itself, this leaves a vast field of meaning to be explored, and it is to this exploration that the English poets have made a significant contribution. Those who have not believed in him, in the conventional way, have still been fascinated by the mystery of this man. So it is not surprising that this fascination finds constant poetic expression. After all, poets deal in the world of meaning and mystery, in the elusive corners of truth. We should expect some of them, at least, to turn their attention to the 'meaning of the mystery', as well as to the 'Mystery of His Meaning'.

The Early Poets

The poets of the middle ages did not question the traditional beliefs about Jesus. Why should they, when the Christian faith was as fundamental to their whole philosophy as the natural law? But they marvelled at the mystery of the man who was both human and divine, and of the love of God which brought him to earth in his Son. The first is simply put in the Middle English parable of the Scapegoat:

For he is certainly divine
True God in nature true;
But he is also man, like us,
In full humanity.

The second theme, the mystery of divine love, is captured beautifully in Piers Plowman's 'Vision of Holy Church', by William Langland:

Then never lighter was a leaf upon a linden tree
Than love was when it took the flesh and blood of man
Fluttering, piercing as a needle point,
No armour can stay it, no, nor high walls.

John Milton, in *Paradise Lost*, imagines Christ addressing his Father, responding to God's invitation to the 'heavenly powers' to rescue fallen humanity by becoming mortal. 'The Heavenly Quire stood mute', but his Son spoke:

Account me Man: I for his sake will leave
Thy bosom, and this glory next to Thee.
Freely put off...

Milton saw the redemption of the world in terms of a cosmic battle, a mighty confrontation between the power of evil and the authority of God himself. George Herbert, from a different poetic tradition, though almost Milton's contemporary, saw it in much more human, much more humbling terms. In his poem 'Redemption' he sought the Lord at his heavenly 'manor', but was told that he had gone to take possession of some land on earth 'which he had dearly bought long since'.

> I straight return'd and, knowing his great birth,
> Sought him accordingly in great resorts;
> In cities, theatres, gardens, parks, and courts;
> At length I heard a ragged noise and mirth
>
> Of thieves and murderers – there I him espied,
> Who straight, 'Your suit is granted', said, and died.

For the early American poet Edward Taylor, the mystery was not so much Jesus as human, but Jesus as 'on his side', Jesus his 'advocate'. He reflected on the words of the first letter of John, 'We have an Advocate with the Father':

> Thou hast the Hint of pleading; plead my State.
> Although it's bad thy Plea will make it best.

He ends with a charming promise:

> If thou wilt plead my Case before the King:
> I'le Waggon Loads of Love, and Glory bring.

The Case Questioned

It wasn't until Blake dipped his mystical pen in the ink of scepticism that English poetry seriously challenged the prevailing orthodoxy of belief about Jesus. In 'The Everlasting Gospel' he set out his own 'vision' of a more human Christ, one freed from the constraints of the Church and its creeds:

> The Vision of Christ that thou dost see
> Is my Vision's Greatest Enemy:
> Thine has a great hook nose like thine,
> Mine has a snub nose like to mine:
> Thine is the friend of All Mankind,
> Mine speaks in parables to the Blind...

There is always the danger of constructing a Christ in our own image, to suit our own needs – one who 'looks like' us. And, Blake argues, this comes from prejudging the Bible's message:

> Both read the Bible day & night,
> But thou reads't black where I read white.

It is the *man* Jesus that Blake values. In the same long poem God addresses his Son:

> Thou art a Man, God is no more,
> Thine own Humanity learn to Adore
> And thy Revenge Abroad display
> In terrors at the Last Judgment day.

Yet those 'terrors' are assuaged by Christ's love, a love which Blake saw in the experience of the woman taken in adultery and brought to Jesus – 'sitting in Moses' chair' – for judgment. For Blake 'Sinai's trumpets ceased to roar' as Jesus revealed the love that surpasses the 'goodness' of the Pharisees, or even of God himself:

> Still the breath Divine does move
> And the breath Divine is Love.

It is probably fruitless to try to create a coherent theology out of Blake's tortured but inspirational mysticism. What he offers are sudden blinding glimpses of truth. The American, John Greenleaf Whittier, writing in the century after Blake, also sits uncomfortably to orthodox creed. Indeed, he feels that men and women have 'deified their hate and selfishness and greed' in 'the pomp of dreadful imagery'. But he has advice for the anxious seeker for the light:

> Let the scared dreamer wake to see
> The Christ of Nazareth at his side!

His contemporary, the doyen of Victorian poets, Tennyson, was not one to attack conventional Christianity head on, but in his great poem of grief, 'In Memoriam', he 'asked the questions'. Addressing, in one section, the 'Strong Son of God', he lays out the dilemma of faith:

> Thou wilt not leave us in the dust:
> Thou madest man, he knows not why;
> He thinks he was not made to die;
> And thou hast made him: thou art just.

It is a genuine cry from the heart, and leaves the poet with faith alone, which he contrasts with the security of 'knowledge':

> We have but faith: we cannot know;
>   For knowledge is of things we see;
>   And yet we trust it comes from thee,
> A beam in darkness: let it grow.

For Tennyson, there is no doubt that this experience of loss challenged his faith (as we saw in an earlier extract from 'In Memoriam', based on the raising of Lazarus). The resurrection is all very well, but those who are bereaved can't wait that long! For other poets of more recent times, their faith problems are less concerned with the acceptance of a widely accepted (but elusive) truth, more a struggle to relate the elusive Jesus to their own experience of life.

Harold Monro, rather like Swinburne in 'Hymn to Proserpine', reflects on the apparent 'sexlessness' of Jesus, imagining a dialogue between the child Cupid, the god of love, and the child Jesus, who was never to marry or experience a sexual relationship:

> Cupid has offered his arrows for Jesus to try;
> He has offered his bow for the game.
> But Jesus went weeping away, and left him there wondering why.

For the Ghanaian poet Kofi Awoonor, it is not Christ's chastity, but the revolutionary impact of his teaching on the ancient traditions of his people that causes him concern. It is 'Easter Dawn', and the shrines of their ancestors are forgotten in the celebration of the resurrection:

> The gods are crying, my father's gods are crying
> for a burial – for a final ritual
> but they that should build the fallen shrines
> have joined the dawn marchers
> singing their way towards Gethsemane...

But still, even for the modern poets, the real problem comes back to that ancient question, 'Who do you say that I am?' It is the identity of Jesus that haunts them, what W.B. Yeats calls 'The uncontrollable mystery on the bestial floor.'

For C. Day Lewis the mystery is summed up in the idea of Jesus as 'the Word' – 'In the beginning was the Word, and the Word was with God, and the Word was God'. Surely God is remote, bound by his own laws to an existence remote from ours:

> They can't get in; but he – for a god no doubt
> Is bound by his own laws – cannot get out.

But, 'the Word was made flesh', moved into 'a precarious air', took a risk that released wonder, dream, vision and prophecy, which were stilled in the heaven of 'Eden'.

For R.S. Thomas it is precisely that issue of the identity of Jesus which is 'The Problem':

> ... Son of God
> or Son of Man? At Jerusalem
> the problem was given a new shape.
> The Cross offered its gaunt solution
> to the Gentiles...

Ted Hughes looked at the same 'problem' through the eyes of Jesus, addressing him as a young man who had struggled with his calling as Son of God:

> ... You did not
> Want to be Christlike. You wanted
> To be with your Father...

And then, in 'Crow Blacker than Ever', Hughes captures the mystery of the incarnation in a powerful, stark couplet:

> So man cried, but with God's voice.
> And God bled, but with man's blood.

There is similarly stark language, but drawing its metaphor from the bull ring (of all places) in Roy Campbell's 'To the Sun'. Christ has many colours, he speculates, the blue water of Galilee, the green of the trees, the gold of palms, the purple of the suffering in Gethsemane. But finally, and triumphantly, there is the red of the Torero:

> Him who took the toss
> And rode the black horns of the cross –
> But rose snow-silver from the dead!

Strangely enough, it is the homely John Betjeman among the modern poets who asks the crucial question. Given all of this mystery, given the struggle to understand who Jesus is and what is the significance of his coming, of his death and resurrection... the question remains, above all –

And is it true? And is it true,
    This most tremendous tale of all…
The Maker of the stars and sea
Become a Child on earth for me?

For 'if it is', he says, then no truth on earth can compare with it.

Yet, as Charles Causley reflects before a Normandy crucifix, for most searchers the issue is seldom as clear-cut as that. Faith demands more than simple intellectual acceptance:

I am the truth, but you will not believe me,
    I am the city where you will not stay…

There is the dilemma of human response. It is plainly *not* for many people simply a question of whether 'it' is 'true' or not. In one of the most perceptive poems on the subject of human response to the mystery of Jesus, 'I am the Way', Alice Meynell reflects on the claim of Jesus to be the Way, and the Truth, and the Life – not only the goal of faith, but its means, too. She is glad that he is the way:

Hadst Thou been nothing but the goal,
    I cannot say
If Thou hadst ever met my soul.

As it is, as a 'child of process', she still has her problems:

    I cannot see –
I, child of process – if there lies
    An end for me,
Full of repose, full of replies.

But her 'feet that err' are still safer on the winding road of faith, where Christ is 'Access, Approach… Time, Way and Wayfarer', than anywhere else.

Her sense is that understanding is less important than travelling. She was a convinced Roman Catholic herself, but for Robert Bridges, in his 'Testament of Beauty', many will 'call him Lord' who neither understand nor obey his commandments:

His kingdom is God's kingdom, and his holy temple
not in Athens or Rome but in the heart of man.
They who understood not cannot forget, and they
who keep not his commandment call him Master and Lord.

The Hidden Key

So the mystery remains a mystery, in the sense of a truth that is beyond mere rationality, though not irrational. Somewhere, the poets seem to feel, there is in the person of Jesus a clue, a key, to what the human situation is all about. For Peter Porter, a contemporary poet, the particular lock into which it fits is the human experience of suffering. There, even reluctantly, we can meet the 'master haunter', Jesus:

> ... I
> am like him, one who cannot
> let go of unhappiness, who has
> come closer to him through suffering
> and loathes the idea...

In his poem, 'The Unlucky Christ', Porter clearly sees Jesus as one whose whole life and meaning is bound up in the universal experience of suffering. But let us give the last word in the introduction to this section to a poet who, one feels, would instinctively *not* agree with Porter. For Stevie Smith, Jesus is not the 'Professional Sorrower' but 'The Airy Christ':

> For he does not wish that men should love him more than
> anything
> Because he died; he only wishes they would hear him sing.

Christ the Cornerstone

O King! Thou art the wall-stone,
which of old the workmen
from their work rejected!
Well it Thee beseemeth
that Thou hold the headship
of this Hall of glory,
and should'st join together
with a fastening firm
the broad-spaced walls
of the flint unbreakable
all fitly framed together;
that among earth's dwellers
all with sight of eyes
may for ever wonder.
O Prince of glory!
now through skill and wisdom
manifest Thy handiwork,
true-fast and firm-set
in sovran splendour.

Cynewulf (9th century),
translated by Ruth Etchells

Homily of the Scapegoat
(see Leviticus 16:5–10)

The two goats signify to us
The two sides of one God.
Our Saviour Jesus Christ himself
Reveals the double truth.
For he is certainly divine
True God in nature true;
But he is also man, like us,
In full humanity.
For Christ is truly God and man,
In rank and nature both,
And to believe this certain truth
God's mercy will release.
One goat was sacrificed to bear
All living people's sin,
As Christ himself bore sin for us,
That we might be forgiven.
He on the cross was crucified,
Nailed there for our need.
So in his true divinity
He saved us from our sin.
But in his true humanity
He drank our cup of pain,
And like the second goat bore off
Man's guilt and agony.

East Midlands (12th century),
translated by David Winter

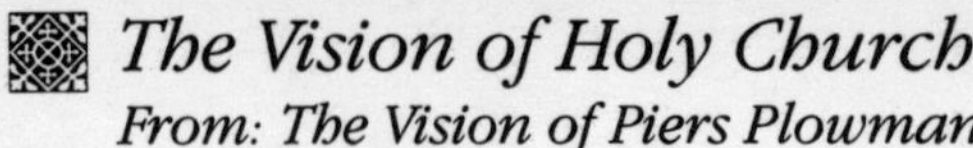

The Vision of Holy Church

From: The Vision of Piers Plowman

Love is the plant of peace,
most precious of all virtues,
Heaven could not hold it,
so heavy was love,
Till it had of this earth
eaten its fill.
Then never lighter was a leaf
upon a linden tree
Than love was when it took
the flesh and blood of man.
Fluttering, piercing
as a needle point,
No armour can stay it,
no, nor high walls.
Therefore is love the leader
of the Lord's folk in heaven
And, as a friend, a mediator
between the King and the people.
Even so Love shapes the law
on man for his misdeeds,
Love lays on man the payment due.

In your heart's conscience
in your deepest well,
In your heart and in your head
the mighty truth be born:
That was the Father's deed,
who made us all,
And looked on us with love,
and let his Son die
Meekly for our misdeeds.

Yet Christ willed no woe
on them that wrought him pain,
With his meek mouth
he prayed for them God's mercy,
For pity on the people
who tortured him to death.

Therefore I counsel you, you rich
have pity on the poor,
Though you are powerful at law
be meek in action;
The same measure you mete
wrong or right,
You shall be meted with
when you go hence.

William Langland (1331–1400),
translated by David Winter

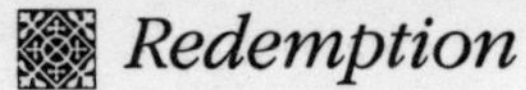

Redemption

Having been tenant long to a rich Lord,
    Not thriving, I resolvèd to be bold,
    And make a suit unto him, to afford
A new small-rented lease, and cancel th'old.

In heaven at his manor I him sought;
    They told me there, that he was lately gone
    About some land, which he had dearly bought
Long since on earth, to take possession.

I straight return'd and, knowing his great birth,
    Sought him accordingly in great resorts;
    In cities, theatres, gardens, parks, and courts;
At length I heard a ragged noise and mirth

    Of thieves and murderers – there I him espied,
    Who straight, 'Your suit is granted', said, and died.

George Herbert (1593–1633)

From: Paradise Lost

'But yet all is not done. Man disobeying,
Disloyal, breaks his fealty, and sins
Against the high supremacy of heaven,
Affecting Godhead, and, so losing all,
To expiate his treason hath naught left,
But, to destruction sacred and devote,
He with his whole posterity must die; –
Die he or Justice must; unless for him
Some other able, and as willing, pay
The rigid satisfaction, death for death.
Say, heavenly powers, where shall we find such love?
Which of ye shall be mortal, to redeem
Man's mortal crime, and just, the unjust to save?
Dwells in all heaven charity so dear?'

He asked, but all the Heavenly Quire stood mute,
And silence was in Heaven: on Man's behalf
Patron or intercessor none appeared –
Much less than durst upon his own head draw
The deadly forfeiture, and ransom set.
And now without redemption all mankind
Must have been lost, adjudged to Death and Hell
By doom severe, had not the Son of God,
In whom the fulness dwells of love divine,
His dearest meditation thus renewed:
'Father, Thy word is passed, Man shall find grace;
And shall Grace not find means, that finds her way,
The speediest of Thy winged messengers,
To visit all Thy creatures, and to all
Comes unprevented, unimplored, unsought?
Happy for Man, so coming! He her aid
Can never seek, once dead in sins and lost –
Atonement for himself, or offering meet,
Indebted and undone, hath none to bring.
Behold Me, then: Me for him, life for life,
I offer; on me let Thine anger fall;
Account Me Man: I for his sake will leave
Thy bosom, and this glory next to Thee.

Freely put off, and for him lastly die
Well pleased; on Me let Death wreak all his rage,
Under his gloomy power I shall not long
Lie vanquished. Thou hast given me to possess
Life in myself for ever; by Thee I live;
Though now to Death I yield, and am his due
All that of me can die, yet, that debt paid,
Thou wilt not leave Me in the loathsome grave
His prey, nor suffer My unspotted soul
For ever with corruption there to dwell;
But I shall rise victorious, and subdue
My vanquisher, spoiled of his vaunted spoil.

John Milton (1608–74)

From: Paradise Regained

So Satan fell; and straight a fiery globe
Of Angels on full sail of wing flew nigh,
Who on their plumy vans received him soft
From his uneasy station, and upbore,
As on a floating couch, through the blithe air;
Then in a flowery valley set Him down
On a green bank, and set before Him spread
A table of celestial food divine
Ambrosial foods fetched from the Tree of Life,
And from the Fount of Life ambrosial drink,
That soon refreshed him wearied, and repaired

What hunger, if aught hunger, had impaired,
Or thirst; and as He fed, Angelic quires
Sung heavenly anthems of His victory
Over temptation and the Tempter proud:
'True Image of the Father, whether throned
In the bosom of bliss, and light of light
Conceiving, or, remote from Heaven, enshrined
In fleshly tabernacle and human form,
Wandering the wilderness – whatever place,
Habit or state or motion still expressing
The Son of God, with Godlike force endued
Against the attempter of Thy Father's throne
And thief of Paradise! Him long of old
Thou didst debel, and down from heaven cast
With all his army; now Thou hast avenged
Supplanted Adam, and by vanquishing
Temptation, hast regained lost Paradise,
And frustrated the conquest fraudulent.
He never more henceforth will dare set foot
In Paradise to tempt; his snares are broke.
For, though that seat of earthly bliss be failed,
A fairer Paradise is founded now
For Adam and his chosen sons, whom Thou,
A Saviour, art come down to reinstall...
Hail, Son of the Most High, heir of both Worlds,
Queller of Satan! On Thy glorious work
Now enter, and begin to save Mankind.'
Thus they the Son of God, our Saviour meek,
Sung victor, and from heavenly feast refreshed,
Brought on His way with joy. He, unobserved,
Home to His mother's house private returned.

John Milton (1608–74)

Meditation: An Advocate with the Father *(1 John 2:1)*

Oh! What a thing is Man? Lord, Who am I?
    That thou shouldst give him Law (Oh! golden Line)
To regulate his Thoughts, Words, Life thereby.
        And judge him Wilt thereby too in thy time.
    A Court of Justice thou in heaven holdst
    To try his Case while he's here housd on mould.

How do thy Angells lay before thine eye
    My Deeds both White, and Black I dayly doe?
How doth thy Court thou Pannellst there them try?
    But flesh complains. What right for this? let's know.
For right, or wrong I can't appeare unto't.
    And shall a sentence Pass on such a suite?

Soft; blemish not this golden Bench, or place.
    Here is no Bribe, nor Colourings to hide
Nor pettifogger to befog the Case
    But Justice hath her Glory here well tri'de.
    Her spotless Law all spotted Cases tends.
Without Respect or Disrespect them ends.

God's Judge himselfe: and Christ Atturny is,
    The Holy Ghost Regesterer is founde.
Angells the sergeants are, all Creatures kiss
    The booke, and doe as Evidences abounde.
    All Cases pass according to pure Law
    And in the sentence is no Fret, nor flaw.

What saist, my soule? Here all thy Deeds are tri'de.
  Is Christ thy Advocate to pleade thy Cause?
Art thou his Client? Such shall never slide.
  He never lost his Case: he pleads such Laws
  As Carry do the same, nor doth refuse
  The Vilest sinners Case that doth him Choose.

This is his Honour, not Dishonour: nay
  No Habeas-Corpus against his Clients came
For all their Fines his Purse doth make down pay.
  He Non-Suites Satan's Suite or Casts the Same.
  He'l plead thy Case, and not accept a Fee.
  He'l plead Sub Forma Pauperis for thee.

My Case is bad. Lord, be my Advocate.
  My sin is red: I'me under God's Arrest.
Thou hast the Hint of pleading; plead my State.
  Although it's bad thy Plea will make it best.
  If thou wilt plead my Case before the King:
  I'le Waggon Loads of Love, and Glory bring.

Edward Taylor (1645–1729)

The Lamb

Little Lamb, who made thee?
Dost thou know who made thee?
Gave thee life, & bid thee feed
By the stream & o'er the mead;
Gave thee clothing of delight,
Softest clothing, wooly, bright;
Gave thee such a tender voice,
Making all the vales rejoice?
Little Lamb, who made thee?
Dost thou know who made thee?

Little Lamb, I'll tell thee,
Little Lamb, I'll tell thee:
He is called by thy name,
For he calls himself a Lamb.
He is meek, & he is mild;
He became a little child.
I a child, & thou a lamb,
We are called by his name.
Little Lamb, God bless thee!
Little Lamb, God bless thee!

William Blake (1757–1827)

What Can this Gospel of Jesus Be?

From: The Everlasting Gospel

What can this Gospel of Jesus be?
What Life & Immortality,
What was it that he brought to Light
That Plato & Cicero did not write?
The Heathen Deities wrote them all,
These Moral Virtues, great & small.
What is the Accusation of Sin
But Moral Virtues' deadly Gin?
The Moral Virtues in their Pride
Did o'er the World triumphant ride
In Wars & Sacrifice for Sin,
And Souls to Hell ran trooping in.
The Accuser, Holy God of All
This Pharisaic Worldly Ball,
Amidst them in his Glory Beams
Upon the Rivers & the Streams.
Then Jesus rose & said to Me,
'Thy Sins are all forgiven thee.'
Loud Pilate Howl'd, loud Caiaphas yell'd,
When they the Gospel Light beheld.
It was when Jesus said to Me,
'Thy Sins are all forgiven thee.'
The Christian trumpets loud proclaim
Thro' all the World in Jesus' name
Mutual forgiveness of each Vice,
And oped the Gates of Paradise.
The Moral Virtues in Great fear
Formed the Cross & Nails & Spear,
And the Accuser standing by
Cried out, 'Crucify! Crucify!
'Our Moral Virtues ne'er can be,
'Nor Warlike pomp & Majesty;
'For Moral Virtues all begin
'In the Accusations of Sin,
'And all the Heroic Virtues End
'In destroying the Sinners' Friend.

'Am I not Lucifer the Great,
'And you my daughters in Great State,
'The fruit of my Mysterious Tree
'Of Good & Evil & Misery
'And Death & Hell, which now begin
'On everyone who Forgives Sin?'

The Vision of Christ that thou dost see
Is my Vision's Greatest Enemy:
Thine has a great hook nose like thine,
Mine has a snub nose like to mine:
Thine is the friend of All Mankind,
Mine speaks in parables to the Blind:
Thine loves the same world that mine hates,
Thy Heaven doors are my Hell Gates.
Socrates taught what Meletus
Loath'd as a Nation's bitterest Curse,
And Caiaphas was in his own Mind
A benefactor to Mankind:
Both read the Bible day & night,
But thou read'st black where I read white.

William Blake (1757–1827)

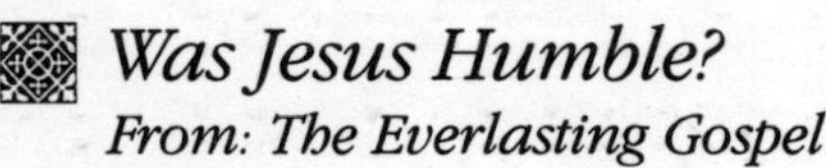

Was Jesus Humble?
From: The Everlasting Gospel

Was Jesus Humble? or did he
Give any proofs of Humility?
When but a Child he ran away
And left his Parents in dismay.
When they had wonder'd three days long
These were the words upon his Tongue:

'No Earthly parents I confess:
'I am doing my Father's business.'
When the rich learned Pharisee
Came to consult him secretly,
Upon his heart with Iron pen
He wrote, 'Ye must be born again.'
He was too Proud to take a bribe;
He spoke with authority, not like a Scribe.
He says with most consummate Art,
'Follow me, I am meek & lowly of heart,'
As that is the only way to Escape
The Miser's net & the Glutton's trap.
He who loves his Enemies, hates his Friends;
This is surely not what Jesus intends;
He must mean the meer love of Civility,
And so he must mean concerning Humility;
But he acts with triumphant, honest pride,
And this is the Reason Jesus died.
If he had been Antichrist, Creeping Jesus,
He'd have done anything to please us;
Gone sneaking into the Synagogues
And not used the Elders & Priests like Dogs,
But humble as a Lamb or an Ass,
Obey himself to Caiaphas.
God wants not Man to humble himself:
This is the Trick of the Ancient Elf.
Humble toward God, Haughty toward Man,
This is the Race that Jesus ran,
And when he humbled himself to God,
Then descended the cruel rod.
'If thou humblest thyself, thou humblest me;
'Thou also dwelst in Eternity.
'Thou art a Man, God is no more,
'Thine own Humanity learn to Adore
'And thy Revenge Abroad display
'In terrors at the Last Judgment day.
'God's Mercy & Long Suffering

'Are but the Sinner to Judgment to bring.
'Thou on the Cross for them shalt pray
'And take Revenge at the last Day.

'Do what you will, this Life's a Fiction
'And is made up of Contradiction.'

William Blake (1757–1827)

Was Jesus Chaste?
From: The Everlasting Gospel

Was Jesus Chaste? or did he
Give any Lessons of Chastity?
The morning blush'd fiery red:
Mary was found in Adulterous bed;
Earth groan'd beneath, & Heaven above
Trembled at discovery of Love.
Jesus was sitting in Moses' Chair,
They brought the trembling Woman There.
Moses commands she be stoned to death,
What was the sound of Jesus' breath?
He laid His hand on Moses' Law:
The Ancient Heavens, in Silent Awe
Writ with Curses from Pole to Pole,
All away began to roll:
The Earth trembling & Naked lay
In secret bed of Mortal Clay,
On Sinai felt the hand divine
Putting back the bloody shrine,
And she heard the breath of God
As she heard by Eden's flood:
'Good & Evil are no more!

'Sinai's trumpets, cease to roar!
'Cease, finger of God, to write!
'The Heavens are not clean in thy Sight.
'Thou art Good, & Thou Alone;
'Nor may the sinner cast one stone.
'To be Good only, is to be
'A God or else a Pharisee.
'Thou Angel of the Presence Divine
'That didst create this Body of Mine,
'Wherefore hast thou writ these Laws
'And Created Hell's dark jaws?
'My Presence I will take from thee:
'A Cold Leper thou shalt be.
'Tho' thou wast so pure & bright
'That Heaven was Impure in thy Sight,
'Tho' thy Oath turn'd Heaven Pale,
'Tho' thy Covenant built Hell's Jail,
'Tho' thou didst all to Chaos roll
'With the Serpent for its soul,
'Still the breath Divine does move
'And the breath Divine is Love.'

William Blake (1757–1827)

From: In Memoriam A.H.H.

Strong Son of God, immortal Love,
  Whom we, that have not seen thy face,
  By faith, and faith alone, embrace,
Believing where we cannot prove;

Thine are these orbs of light and shade;
  Thou madest Life in man and brute;
  Thou madest Death; and lo, thy foot
Is on the skull which thou hast made.

Thou wilt not leave us in the dust:
  Thou madest man, he knows not why;
  He thinks he was not made to die;
And thou hast made him: thou art just.

Thou seemest human and divine,
  The highest, holiest manhood, thou:
  Our wills are ours, we know not how;
Our wills are ours, to make them thine.

Our little systems have their day;
  They have their day and cease to be:
  They are but broken lights of thee,
And thou, O Lord, art more than they.

We have but faith: we cannot know;
  For knowledge is of things we see;
  And yet we trust it comes from thee,
A beam in darkness: let it grow.

Let knowledge grow from more to more,
  But more of reverence in us dwell;
  That mind and soul, according well,
May make one music as before,

But vaster. We are fools and slight;
  We mock thee when we do not fear:
  But help thy foolish ones to bear;
Help thy vain worlds to bear thy light.

Forgive what seem'd my sin in me;
  What seem'd my worth since I began;
  For merit lives from man to man,
And not from man, O Lord, to thee.

Forgive my grief for one removed,
  Thy creature, whom I found so fair.
  I trust he lives in thee, and there
I find him worthier to be loved.

Forgive these wild and wandering cries,
  Confusions of a wasted youth;
  Forgive them where they fail in truth,
And in thy wisdom make me wise.

Alfred, Lord Tennyson (1809–92)

The Over-Heart

For of Him, and through Him, and to Him are all things: to whom be glory forever! (Romans 11:36)

Fade, pomp of dreadful imagery
  Wherewith mankind have deified
  Their hate, and selfishness, and pride!
Let the scared dreamer wake to see
  The Christ of Nazareth at his side!

What doth that holy Guide require?
  No rite of pain, nor gift of blood,
  But man a kindly brotherhood,
Looking, where duty is desire,
  To Him, the beautiful and good.

Gone be the faithlessness of fear,
  And let the pitying heaven's sweet rain
  Wash out the altar's bloody stain;
The law of Hatred disappear,
  The law of Love alone remain.

How fall the idols false and grim!
  And lo! their hideous wreck above
  The emblems of the Lamb and Dove!
Man turns from God, not God from him;
  And guilt, in suffering, whispers Love!

The world sits at the feet of Christ,
  Unknowing, blind, and unconsoled;
  It yet shall touch His garment's fold,
And feel the heavenly Alchemist
  Transform its very dust to gold.

The theme befitting angel tongues
  Beyond a mortal's scope has grown.
  O heart of mine! with reverence own
The fulness which to it belongs,
And trust the unknown for the known.

John Greenleaf Whittier (1807–92)

 *From: The Testament of Beauty*

So it was when Jesus came in his gentleness
with his divine compassion and great Gospel of Peace,
men hail'd him WORD OF GOD, and in the title of Christ
crown'd him with love beyond all earth-names of renown.
For He, wandering unarm'd save by the Spirit's flame,
in few years with few friends founded a world-empire
wider than Alexander's and more enduring;
since from his death it took its everlasting life.
His kingdom is God's kingdom, and his holy temple
not in Athens or Rome but in the heart of man.
They who understood not cannot forget, and they
who keep not his commandment call him Master and Lord.
He preach'd once to the herd, but now calleth the wise,
and shall in his second Advent, that tarried long,
be glorified by the Greeks that come to the feast:
But the great Light shineth in great darkness, the seed
that fell by the wayside hath been trodden under foot,
that which fell on the Rock is nigh wither'd away;
While louder and louder thro' the dazed head of the
SPHINX the old lion's voice roareth o'er the lands.

Robert Bridges (1844–1930)

I am the Way

Thou art the Way.
Hadst Thou been nothing but the goal,
I cannot say
If Thou hadst ever met my soul.

I cannot see –
I, child of process – if there lies
An end for me,
Full of repose, full of replies.

I'll not reproach
The road that winds, my feet that err.
Access, Approach
Art Thou, Time, Way, and Wayfarer.

Alice Meynell (1847–1922)

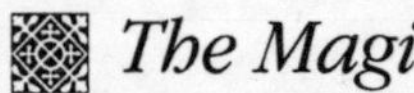

The Magi

Now as at all times I can see in the mind's eye,
In their stiff, painted clothes, the pale unsatisfied ones
Appear and disappear in the blue depth of the sky
With all their ancient faces like rain-beaten stones,
And all their helms of silver hovering side by side,
And all their eyes still fixed, hoping to find once more,
Being by Calvary's turbulence unsatisfied,
The uncontrollable mystery on the bestial floor.

W.B. Yeats (1865–1939)

Children of Love

The holy boy
Went from his mother out in the cool of the day
Over the sun-parched fields
And in among the olives shining green and shining grey.

There was no sound,
No smallest voice of any shivering stream.
Poor sinless little boy,
He desired to play, and to sing; he could only sigh and dream.

Suddenly came
Running along to him naked, with curly hair,
That rogue of the lovely world,
That other beautiful child whom the virgin Venus bare.

The holy boy
Gazed with those sad blue eyes that all men know.
Impudent Cupid stood
Panting, holding an arrow and pointing his bow.

('Will you not play?
Jesus, run to him, run to him, swift for our joy.
Is he not holy, like you?
Are you afraid of his arrows, O beautiful dreaming boy?')

And now they stand
Watching one another with timid gaze;
Youth has met youth in the wood,
But holiness will not change its melancholy ways.

Cupid at last
Draws his bow and softly lets fly a dart.
Smile for a moment, sad world! –
It has grazed the white skin and drawn blood from the sorrowful heart.

Now, for delight,
Cupid tosses his locks and goes wantonly near;
But the child that was born to the cross
Has let fall on his cheek, for the sadness of life, a compassionate tear.

Marvellous dream!
Cupid has offered his arrows for Jesus to try;
He has offered his bow for the game.
But Jesus went weeping away, and left him there wondering why.

Harold Monro (1879–1932)

 *In the Beginning was the Word*

In the beginning was the Word.
Under different skies now, I recall
The childhood of the Word.
Before the Fall,
Was dancing on the green with sun and moon:
And the Word was with God.
Years pass, relaxed in a faun's afternoon.
And the Word was God.
For him rise up the litanies of leaves
From the tormented wood, and semi-breves
Of birds accompany the simple dawn.
Obsequious to his mood the valleys yawn,
Nymphs scamper or succumb, waterfalls part
The hill-face with vivacious smiles. The heart,
Propped up against its paradise, records
Each wave of godhead in a sea of words.
He grows a wall of sunflower and moonflower blent
To protest his solitude and to prevent
Wolf or worm from trespassing on his rule.
Observe how paradise can make a fool:
They can't get in; but he – for a god no doubt
Is bound by his own laws – cannot get out.
And the Word was made flesh,
Under different skies now,
Wrenching a stony song from a scant acre,
The Word still justifies its Maker.

Green fields were my slippers,
    Sky was my hat,
But curiosity
    Killed the cat.
For this did I burst
    My daisy band –
To be clapped in irons
    By a strange hand?
Nevertheless, you are well out of Eden:
For there's no wonder where all things are new;
No dream where all is sleep; no vision where
Seer and seen are one; nor prophecy
Where only echo waits upon the tongue.
    Now he has come to a country of stone walls.
Breathes a precarious air.
Frontiers of adamant declare
A cold autonomy. There echo starves;
And the mountain ash breathes stoically there
Above the muscular stream.
What cairn will show the way he went?
A harrow rusting on defeated bones?
Or will he leave a luckier testament –
Rock deeply rent,
Fountains of spring playing upon the air?

C. Day Lewis (1904–72)

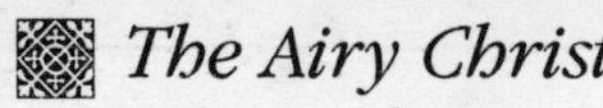

The Airy Christ

(After reading Dr Rieu's translation of St Mark's Gospel)

Who is this that comes in splendour, coming from the blazing East?
This is he we had not thought of, this is he the airy Christ.

Airy, in an airy manner in an airy parkland walking,
Others take him by the hand, lead him, do the talking.

But the Form, the airy One, frowns an airy frown,
What they say he knows must be, but he looks aloofly down.

Looks aloofly at his feet, looks aloofly at his hands,
Knows they must, as prophets say, nailèd be to wooden bands,

As he knows the words he sings, that he sings so happily
Must be changed to working laws, yet sings he ceaselessly.

Those who truly hear the voice, the words, the happy song,
Never shall need working laws to keep from doing wrong.

Deaf men will pretend sometimes they hear the song, the words,
And make excuse to sin extremely; this will be absurd.

Heed it not. Whatever foolish men may do the song is cried
For those who hear, and the sweet singer does not care that he
was crucified.

For he does not wish that men should love him more than
anything
Because he died; he only wishes they would hear him sing.

Stevie Smith (1902–71)

Judas Iscariot

Judas Iscariot
    sat in the upper
    room with the others
    at the last supper

And sitting there smiled
    up at his master
    whom he knew the morrow
    would roll in disaster.

At Christ's look he guffawed –
    for then as thereafter
    Judas was greatly
    given to laughter.

Indeed they always said
    that he was the veriest
    prince of good fellows
    and the whitest and merriest.

All the days of his life
    he lived gay as a cricket
    and would sing like the thrush
    that sings in the thicket

He would sing like the thrush
    that sings on the thorn
    oh he was the most sporting bird
    that ever was born.

R.A.K. Mason (1905–71)

Christmas

The bells of waiting Advent ring,
    The Tortoise stove is lit again
And lamp-oil light across the night
    Has caught the streaks of winter rain
In many a stained-glass window sheen
From Crimson Lake to Hooker's Green.

The holly in the windy hedge
    And round the Manor House the yew
Will soon be stripped to deck the ledge,
    The altar, font and arch and pew,
So that the villagers can say
'The church looks nice' on Christmas Day.

Provincial public houses blaze
    And Corporation tramcars clang,
On lighted tenements I gaze
    Where paper decorations hang,
And bunting in the red Town Hall
Says 'Merry Christmas to you all'.

And London shops on Christmas Eve
    Are strung with silver bells and flowers
As hurrying clerks the City leave
    To pigeon-haunted classic towers,
And marbled clouds go scudding by
The many-steepled London sky.

And girls in slacks remember Dad,
    And oafish louts remember Mum,
And sleepless children's hearts are glad,
    And Christmas-morning bells say 'Come!'
Even to shining ones who dwell
Safe in the Dorchester Hotel.

And is it true? And is it true,
    This most tremendous tale of all,
Seen in a stained-glass window's hue,
    A Baby in an ox's stall?
The Maker of the stars and sea
Become a Child on earth for me?

And is it true? For if it is,
    No loving fingers tying strings
Around those tissued fripperies,
    The sweet and silly Christmas things,
Bath salts and inexpensive scent
And hideous tie so kindly meant,

No love that in a family dwells,
    No carolling in frosty air,
Nor all the steeple-shaking bells
    Can with this single Truth compare –
That God was Man in Palestine
And lives to-day in Bread and Wine.

John Betjeman (1906–84)

The Hand

It was a hand. God looked at it
and looked away. There was a coldness
about his heart, as though the hand
clasped it. As at the end
of a dark tunnel, he saw cities
the hand would build, engines
that it would raze them with. His sight
dimmed. Tempted to undo the joints
of the fingers, he picked it up.
But the hand wrestled with him. 'Tell
me your name,' it cried, 'and I will write it
in bright gold. Are there not deeds
to be done, children to make, poems
to be written? The world
is without meaning, awaiting
my coming.' But God, feeling the nails
in his side, the unnerving warmth
of the contact, fought on in
silence. This was the long war with himself
always foreseen, the question not
to be answered. What is the hand
for? The immaculate conception
preceding the delivery
of the first tool? 'I let you go,'
he said, 'but without blessing.
Messenger to the mixed things
of your making, tell them I am.'

R.S. Thomas (1913–)

The Interrogation

But the financiers will ask
in that day: Is it not better
to leave broken bank balances
behind us than broken heads?

And Christ recognizing the
new warriors will feel breaching
his healed side their terrible
pencil and the haemorrhage of its figures.

R.S. Thomas (1913–)

The Problem

There was this problem.
The mind contemplated it;
the body amused itself
in the sun. Put it by, put it by,
the wind whispered. The mind
dozed. Seven empires went under
the blown sand. A people stood up
in Athens; the problem recognized
them, but was not to be outstared
by their blind sculpture. Son of God
or Son of Man? At Jerusalem
the problem was given a new shape.
The Cross offered its gaunt solution
to the Gentiles; under its shadow
their bones whitened. The philosophers christened
their premise. The problem reposed
over the cellars of the alchemists.

R.S. Thomas (1913–)

The Unlucky Christ

Wherever they put down roots
he will be there, the Master-Haunter
who is our sample and our
would-be deliverer. Argue this –
there were men before him,
as there were dreams before events,
as there is (or perhaps is not)
conservation of energy. So he
is out of time but once stopped here
in time. What I am thinking
may be blasphemy, that I
am like him, one who cannot
let go of unhappiness, who has
come closer to him through suffering
and loathes the idea. The ego now,
that must be like a ministry,
the sense of being chosen among men
to be acquainted with grief!
Why not celebrate instead
the wayside cactus which enriches
the air with a small pink flower,
a lovely gift to formalists?

Some people can take straight off
from everyday selfishness to
the mystical, but the vague shape
of the Professional Sorrower
seems to interpose when I try
such transport. The stone had to roll
and the cerements sit up
because he would have poisoned
the world. It has been almost possible
to get through this poem without writing
the word death. The smallest
of our horrors. When they saw him
again upon the road, at least they knew
that the task of misery would be
explained, the evangelical duty
properly underlined. Tell them
about bad luck, he said,
how people who get close to you
want to walk out on you,
tell them they may meet one person
even more shrouded than themselves.
Jesus's message at Pentecost
sounded as our news always does,
that there is eloquence and decency,
but as for happiness,
it is involuntary like hell.

Peter Porter (1929–)

To the Sun

O let your shining orb grow dim,
Of Christ the mirror and the shield,
That I may gaze through you to Him,
See half the miracle revealed,
And in your seven hues behold
The Blue Man walking on the sea;
The Green, beneath the summer tree,
Who called the children; then the Gold,
with palms; the Orange, flaring bold
with scourges; Purple in the garden
(As Greco saw); and then the Red
Torero (Him who took the toss
And rode the black horns of the cross –
But rose snow-silver from the dead!)

Roy Campbell (1901–57)

I am the Great Sun

(From: A Normandy Crucifix of 1632)

I am the great sun, but you do not see me,
    I am your husband, but you turn away.
I am the captive, but you do not free me,
    I am the captain you will not obey.

I am the truth, but you will not believe me,
    I am the city where you will not stay,
I am your wife, your child, but you will leave me,
    I am that God to whom you will not pray.

I am your counsel, but you do not hear me,
    I am the lover whom you will betray,
I am the victor, but you do not cheer me,
    I am the holy dove whom you will slay.

I am your life, but you will not name me,
Seal up your soul with tears, and never blame me.

Charles Causley (1917–)

Crow Blacker than Ever

When God, disgusted with man,
Turned towards Heaven,
And man, disgusted with God,
Turned towards Eve,
Things looked like falling apart.

But Crow Crow
Crow nailed them together,
Nailing Heaven and earth together –

So man cried, but with God's voice.
And God bled, but with man's blood.

Then Heaven and earth creaked at the joint
Which became gangrenous and stank –
A horror beyond redemption.

The agony did not diminish.

Man could not be man nor God God.

The agony

Grew.

Crow

Grinned

Crying: 'This is my Creation,'

Flying the black flag of himself.

Ted Hughes (1930–)

Being Christlike

You did not want to be Christlike. Though your Father
Was your God and there was no other, you did not
Want to be Christlike. Though you walked
In the love of your Father. Though you stared
At the stranger your Mother.
What had she to do with you
But tempt you from your Father?
When her great hooded eyes lowered
Their moon so close
Promising the earth you saw
Your fate and you cried
Get thee behind me. You did not
Want to be Christlike. You wanted
To be with your Father
In wherever he was. And your body
Barred your passage. And your family
Which were your flesh and blood
Burdened it. And a god
That was not your Father
Was a false god. But you did not
Want to be Christlike.

Ted Hughes (1930–)

Easter Dawn

That man died in Jerusalem
And his death demands dawn marchers
From year to year to the sound of bells.
The hymns flow through the mornings
Heard on Calvary this dawn.
The gods are crying, my father's gods are crying
for a burial – for a final ritual –
but they that should build the fallen shrines
have joined the dawn marchers
singing their way towards Gethsemane
where the tear drops of agony still freshen the cactus.
He has risen! Christ has risen!
the gods cried again from the hut in me
asking why that prostration has gone unheeded.
The marchers sang of the resurrection
That concerned the hillock of Calvary
Where the ground at the foot of the cross is level.
the gods cried, shedding
clayey tears on the calico
the drink offering had dried up in the harmattan
the cola-nut is shrivelled
the yam feast has been eaten by mice
and the fetish priest is dressing for the Easter service.
The resurrection hymns come to me from afar
touching my insides.
Then the gods cried loudest
Challenging the hymners.
They seized their gongs and drums
And marched behind the dawn marchers
Seeking their Calvary
Seeking their tombstones
And those who refused to replace them
In the appropriate season.

Kofi Awoonor (1935–)

s e v e n

Beyond the Present

It is easy to think of Christianity as a religion deeply rooted in the past. After all, its defining beliefs are about certain events which are claimed to be part of the history of the human race: the teaching, life, death and resurrection of Jesus Christ nearly 2,000 years ago. Most of the Christian Creed is taken up by the recital of those events: 'Born of the Virgin Mary, suffered under Pontius Pilate, was crucified, dead and buried...'

Yet even in the Creed there is another note, one which in the early days of Christianity was the truly defining one: 'He will come again in glory to judge the living and the dead, and his kingdom will have no end.' That was the 'blessed hope' which shaped the life of the first Christians, living as they did in daily, hourly expectation of Christ's second coming.

Of course, it *didn't* come in those early days. By the time the second letter of Peter was written – towards the end of the first century – the voice of scepticism is being raised: 'Where is the promise of his coming? For ever since our ancestors died, all things continue as they were from the beginning of creation.' So spoke what the writer called 'the scoffers'. And his answer was to remind them that 'with the Lord one day is like a thousand years, and a thousand years are like a day'. The Church took his message to heart, and in effect turned an urgent and immediate hope into a long-term article of the faith, one recited Sunday by Sunday in the liturgy ('Christ will come again...') but seldom proclaimed as a central element of the faith.

Yet, there it is, part of the Christian 'case', non-negotiable in terms of the teaching of Jesus, for whom it was of major importance, not at all a peripheral or theoretical doctrine. He would leave his disciples, he told them, and would 'come again', on the great and terrible 'Day of the Lord', to bring in God's reign of justice, peace and holiness.

The Poets and the Distant Scene

In the everyday world of work and commerce and child-rearing and sheer daily survival the 'distant scene' has usually been exactly that – distant. Yet present lives are undoubtedly shaped by what we believe about that 'distant scene', whether that belief is in the extinction of personality or in its glorious fulfilment in some divine purpose. Poets tend to deal in distant scenes, often alongside present concerns. It's part of seeing things as a whole. That is perhaps why they have seldom shared in the general apathy about what we might call 'ultimate questions'. For the poet, where we come from shapes our present, and where we are going (if anywhere) shapes our future. So the poets who have written about things 'beyond the present' have not done so simply because of a philosophical interest in the subject, but because how we think about the future affects our lives here and now.

The Early Poets

For the early poets, as on other subjects, the traditional Catholic teaching was their starting point. For some, like William Langland in 'The Harrowing of Hell', the second coming was good news for some, as they imagined the host of the redeemed pouring up from the grave into the bliss of eternal life:

> And along that light all those
> Our Lord loved came streaming out.

But what was good news for some was distinctly *not* good news for others. The early American poet Michael Wigglesworth, writing in the seventeenth century from a Puritan background, has a dire warning for the 'vile wretches' who 'stopt their ear and would not hear, when Mercy warned them':

> Now Atheist blind, whose brutish mind
>   a God could never see,
> Dost thou perceive, dost now believe,
>   that Christ thy Judge shall be?

Wigglesworth's contemporary in England, Henry Vaughan, was similarly concerned to urge his readers to 'leave their foolish ranges' before it was too late, but the incentive was a gentler one:

> If thou canst get but thither,
> There growes the flowre of peace,
> The Rose that cannot wither,
> Thy fortresse, and thy ease…

For Vaughan, the crucial test was not for others, but for himself. Would *he* be 'ready' to face the coming of Christ as his Judge? In his poem 'The Dawning' his prayer is for that 'readiness':

> ... let my course, my aim, my love
> And chief acquaintance be above...

Then –

> Thou'lt find me dressed and on my way
> Watching the break of thy great day.

The Modern Mind

With the dawning of a less conventionally religious age, the poets of the last century have not felt bound by what many of them would have seen as dire dogmas of the age of faith. Yet the apocalyptic events of their period have awakened in several of them a keen awareness of the relevance of the same themes of judgment, justice and the destiny of all.

W.B. Yeats combined a passionate involvement in the political turmoil of his beloved Ireland – he was a senator in the Irish Free State in the 1920s – with a fascination for mysticism and the occult. Yet it was to the language of the classical Christian doctrines of the 'end times' that he turned when despair at the state of things overwhelmed him:

> Things fall apart; the centre cannot hold;
> Mere anarchy is loosed upon the world...

And what might that presage?

> Surely some revelation is at hand;
> Surely the Second Coming is at hand.

In contrast, the horrors of the First World War drove Wilfred Owen to the conclusion that the 'Christian Hope' was baseless:

> Of a truth
> All death will He annul, all tears assuage?

His question evokes unbelief from those who have lived longest: 'When I do ask white Age he saith not so', and when he asks 'the earth', she replies:

> Mine ancient scars shall not be glorified,
> Nor my titanic tears, the sea, be dried.

Alice Meynell, who also lived through the First World War, did not find her Christian faith threatened by its horrors. Nor was it shaken by the fast-unfolding discoveries of modern science. On the contrary. If the universe is as vast and varied as the new discoveries suggested, then God's plans for it must be equally vast and varied – including, she suggests in her poem 'Christ in the Universe', a multiplication of incarnations, the wonder of which we shall only be able to comprehend 'in the eternities':

Doubtless we shall compare together, hear
A million alien Gospels, in what guise
He trod the Pleiades, the Lyre, the Bear.

Hugh MacDiarmid, in 'The Innumerable Christ', reflects on much the same idea – 'other stars may have their Bethlehems, and their Calvary too'. Long before the days of space travel, the poets were speculating on its relevance for our understanding of God and his ways with us.

Death as the Future Present

For many Christians in the modern era the 'second coming' of Christ is the moment of death, the point at which we make our own rendezvous with the Saviour and Judge of all. For Evangeline Paterson, in her poem 'Deathbed', this is the moment when we move from our 'lighted present/ into the trackless dark'. In that moment, it is not the image of the Son of God 'coming with great glory in the clouds of heaven' that brings comfort, but the homelier Christ of Galilee and Easter morning:

We turn, blinded,
Not to the Christ in glory,
Stars about his feet,

But to the Son of Man,
Back from the tomb…

Clues from the Natural World

Finally, a word about two modern poets, one British, the other Nigerian, who find clues about the 'distant scene' from the natural world. Christopher Okigbo looks at the Passion Flower, with its graphic images of the suffering Jesus, 'him who was silenced':

whose advent
dumb bells in the dim light celebrate
with wine song...

The flower speaks of tears, of the light of the world and of penitence, and of one who came and who comes:

Messiah will come again,
After the argument in heaven;
Messiah will come again...

John Burnside takes the revelation of nature much further. In his poem 'Parousia' (the New Testament Greek word for the 'appearing' of Christ) he finds clues to the nature of that appearing in the intimacy of ordinary things and in the eternal survival of life in the midst of death. It is not, for him, the great, cataclysmic climax of history, but something more elusive, and closer to our understanding of the way things are:

– but I think, if it came, there would be
something more subtle:
a blur at the corner of vision, a trick of the light,
or the notion that things have shifted

closer...

He 'squats in the fen-smell' to experience –

... the sub-microscopic
pattern of resurrection.

But there is more, much more – after all, the Christ who appears is the Christ who has already appeared once, and suffered like us, and died:

but somewhere along the way
I would meet the Christ:
a tripwire; a mat of hair; an open wound;
the silver of fish blood and bone
in the whites of his eyes.

This seems a long way from William Langland, or Vaughan, or Wigglesworth, but then the twenty-first century is a long way from the fourteenth. Yet Meynell and Okigbo and Burnside have only done what poets always do, and which their ancient forebears would surely approve. They have taken an old truth, turned it this way and that, and found ways to connect it with the reality of their present situation. 'Christ will come again' is still the hope, but the stage on which he will appear is so very, very different.

The Harrowing of Hell
From: The Vision of Piers Plowman

Again
The light said unlock:
Said Lucifer, Who
Goes there?
A huge voice replied, the lord
Of power, of strength, that made
All things. Dukes of this dark place
Undo these gates so Christ come
In, the son of heaven's King.
With that word, hell split apart,
Burst its devil's bars; no man
Nor guard could stop the gates swing
Wide. The old religious men,
Prophets, people who had walked
In darkness, 'Behold the Lamb
Of God', with Saint John sang now.
But Lucifer could not look
At it, the light blinding him.
And along that light all those
Our Lord loved came streaming out.

William Langland (1331–1400),
translated by Ronald Tamplin

Advent

I saw him with flesh all be-spread: He came from East.
I saw him with blood all be-shed: He came from West.
I saw that many he with him brought: He came from South.
I saw that the world of him ne rought: He came from North.

'I come from the wedlock as a sweet spouse that have my
    wife with me y-nome.
I come from fight as a stalwart knight that my foe have
    overcome.
I come from the cheaping as a rich chapman that
    mankind have y-bought.
I come from an uncouth land as a silly pilgrim that
    far have y-sought.'

Anonymous (14th century)

The Dawning

Ah! what time wilt thou come? when shall that cry,
    'The Bridegroom's coming!' fill the sky?
    Shall it in the evening run
    When our words and works are done?
    Or will thy all-surprising light
        Break at midnight,
    When either sleep or some dark pleasure
    Possesseth mad man without measure?
    Or shall these early fragrant hours
        Unlock thy bowers,
    And with their blush of light descry
    Thy locks crowned with eternity?
    Indeed it is the only time
    That with thy glory doth best chime:
    All now are stirring, every field
        Full hymns doth yield,
    The whole creation shakes off night,
    And for thy shadow looks the light;
    Stars now vanish without number,
    Sleepy planets set, and slumber,
    The pursy clouds disband, and scatter;
    All expect some sudden matter,
    Not one beam triumphs, but from far
        That morning-star.

O at what time soever thou,
Unknown to us, the heavens wilt bow,
And with thy angels in the van
Descend to judge poor careless man,
Grant, I may not like puddle lie
In a corrupt security
Where, if a traveller water crave,
He finds it dead, and in a grave.
But as this restless vocal spring
All day and night doth run, and sing,
And though here born, yet is acquainted
Elsewhere, and flowing keeps untainted;
So let me all my busy age
In thy free services engage,
And though, while here, of force I must
Have commerce sometimes with poor dust,
And in my flesh, though vile, and low,
As this doth in her channel flow,
Yet let my course, my aim, my love
And chief acquaintance be above;
So when that day and hour shall come
In which thyself will be the sun,
Thou'lt find me dressed and on my way
Watching the break of thy great day.

Henry Vaughan (1622–95)

Peace

My Soul, there is a Countrie
    Far beyond the stars,
Where stands a winged Sentrie
    All skilfull in the wars,
There above noise, and danger
    Sweet peace sits crown'd with smiles,
And one born in a Manger
    Commands the Beauteous files,
He is thy gracious friend,
    And (O my Soul awake!)
Did in pure love descend
    To die here for thy sake,
If thou canst get but thither,
    There growes the flowre of peace,
The Rose that cannot wither,
    Thy fortresse, and thy ease;
Leave then thy foolish ranges;
    For none can thee secure,
But one, who never changes,
    Thy God, thy life, thy Cure.

Henry Vaughan (1622–95)

Preparations

Yet if His Majesty, our sovereign lord,
Should of his own accord
Friendly himself invite,
And say, 'I'll be your guest to-morrow night,'
How should we stir ourselves, call and command
All hands to work! 'Let no man idle stand!
Set me fine Spanish tables in the hall,
See they be fitted all;
Let there be room to eat,
And order taken that there want no meat;
See every sconce and candlestick made bright,
That without tapers they may give a light.
Look to the presence; are the carpets spread,
The dazie o'er the head,
The cushions in the chairs,
And all the candles lighted on the stairs?
Perfume the chambers, and in any case
Let each man give attendance in his place!'
Thus if a king were coming would we do,
And, 'twere good reason too;
For 'tis a duteous thing
To show all honour to an earthly king,
And after all our travail and our cost,
So he be pleased, to think no labour lost.
But at the coming of the King of Heaven
All's set at six and seven:
We wallow in our sin,
Christ cannot find a chamber in the inn,
We entertain Him always like a stranger,
And, as at first, still lodge Him in a manger.

Anonymous (17th century)

From: The Day of Doom

Still was the night, Serene and Bright,
 when all Men sleeping lay;
Calm was the season, and carnal reason
 thought so 'twould last for ay.
Soul, take thine ease, let sorrow cease,
 much good thou hast in store:
This was their Song, their Cups among,
 the Evening before.

Wallowing in all kind of sin,
 vile wretches lay secure:
The best of men had scarcely then
 their Lamps kept in good ure,
Virgins unwise, who through disguise
 amongst the best were number'd,
Had clos'd their eyes; yea, and the wise
 through sloth and frailty slumber'd.

Like as of old, when Men grow bold
 Gods threatnings to contemn,
Who stopt their Ear, and would not hear,
 when Mercy warned them:
But took their course, without remorse,
 til God began to powre
Destruction the World upon
 in a tempestuous showre.

They put away the evil day,
 and drown'd their care and fears,
Till drown'd were they, and swept away
 by vengeance unawares:
So at the last, whilst Men sleep fast
 in their security,
Surpriz'd they are in such a snare
 as cometh suddenly.

For at midnight brake forth a Light,
 which turn'd the night to day,
And speedily an hideous cry
 did all the world dismay.
Sinners awake, their hearts do ake,
 trembling their loynes surprizeth;
Amaz'd with fear, by what they hear,
 each one of them ariseth.

They rush from Beds with giddy heads,
 and to their windows run,
Viewing this light, which shines more bright
 then doth the Noon-day Sun.
Straightway appears (they see't with tears)
 the Son of God most dread;
Who with his Train comes on amain
 To Judge both Quick and Dead.

Before his face the Heav'ns gave place,
 and Skies are rent asunder,
With mighty voice, and hideous noise,
 more terrible than Thunder.
His brightness damps heav'ns glorious lamps
 and makes them hide their heads,
As if afraid and quite dismay'd,
 they quit their wonted steads.

Ye sons of men that durst contemn
 the Threatnings of Gods Word,
How cheer you now? your hearts, I trow,
 are thrill'd as with a sword.
Now Atheist blind, whose brutish mind
 a God could never see,
Dost thou perceive, dost now believe,
 that Christ thy Judge shall be?

Michael Wigglesworth (1631–1705)

St Agnes' Eve

Deep on the convent-roof the snows
Are sparkling to the moon:
My breath to heaven like vapour goes:
May my soul follow soon!
The shadows of the convent-towers
Slant down the snowy sward,
Still creeping with the creeping hours
That lead me to my Lord:
Make Thou my spirit pure and clear
As are the frosty skies,
Or this first snowdrop of the year
That in my bosom lies.

As these white robes are soil'd and dark,
To yonder shining ground;
As this pale taper's earthly spark,
To yonder argent round;
So shows my soul before the Lamb,
My spirit before Thee;
So in mine earthly house I am,
To that I hope to be.
Break up the heavens, O Lord! and far,
Thro' all yon starlight keen,
Draw me, thy bride, a glittering star,
In raiment white and clean.

He lifts me to the golden doors;
The flashes come and go;
All heaven bursts her starry floors,
And strows her lights below,
And deepens on and up! the gates
Roll back, and far within
For me the Heavenly Bridegroom waits,
To make me pure of sin.
The sabbaths of Eternity,
One sabbath deep and wide –
A light upon the shining sea –
The Bridegroom with his bride!

Alfred, Lord Tennyson (1809–92)

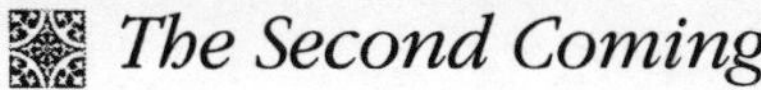

The Second Coming

Turning and turning in the widening gyre
The falcon cannot hear the falconer;
Things fall apart; the centre cannot hold;
Mere anarchy is loosed upon the world,
The blood-dimmed tide is loosed, and everywhere
The ceremony of innocence is drowned;
The best lack all conviction, while the worst
Are full of passionate intensity.

Surely some revelation is at hand;
Surely the Second Coming is at hand.
The Second Coming! Hardly are those words out
When a vast image out of *Spiritus Mundi*
Troubles my sight: somewhere in sands of the desert
A shape with lion body and the head of a man,
A gaze blank and pitiless as the sun,
Is moving its slow thighs, while all about it
Reel shadows of the indignant desert birds.
The darkness drops again; but now I know
That twenty centuries of stony sleep
Were vexed to nightmare by a rocking cradle,
And what rough beast, its hour come round at last,
Slouches towards Bethlehem to be born?

W.B. Yeats (1865–1939)

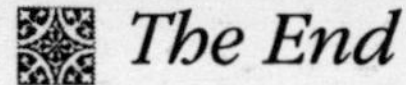

The End

After the blast of lightning from the East,
The flourish of loud clouds, the Chariot Throne;
After the drums of Time have rolled and ceased,
And by the bronze west long retreat is blown,

Shall life renew these bodies? Of a truth
All death will He annul, all tears assuage? –
Fill the void veins of Life again with youth,
And wash, with an immortal water, Age?

When I do ask white Age he saith not so:
'My head hangs weighed with snow.'
And when I hearken to the Earth, she saith:
'My fiery heart shrinks, aching. It is death.
Mine ancient scars shall not be glorified,
Nor my titanic tears, the sea, be dried.'

Wilfred Owen (1893–1918)

Christ in the Universe

With this ambiguous earth
His dealings have been told us. These abide:
The signal to a maid, and human birth,
The lesson, and the young Man crucified.

But not a star of all
The innumerable host of stars has heard
How He administered this terrestrial ball.
Our race have kept their Lord's entrusted Word.

Of His earth-visiting feet
None knows the secret, cherished, perilous,
The terrible, shamefast, frightened, whispered, sweet,
Heart-shattering secret of His way with us.

No planet knows that this
Our wayside planet, carrying land and wave,
Love and life multiplied, and pain and bliss,
Bears, as chief treasure, one forsaken grave.

Nor, in our little day,
May His devices with the heavens be guessed,
His pilgrimage to thread the Milky Way
Or his bestowals there be manifest.

But in the eternities,
Doubtless we shall compare together, hear
A million alien Gospels, in what guise
He trod the Pleiades, the Lyre, the Bear.

O, be prepared, my soul!
To read the inconceivable, to scan
The million forms of God those stars unroll
When, in our turn, we show to them a Man.

Alice Meynell (1847–1922)

The Innumerable Christ

'Other stars may have their Bethlehem, and their Calvary too' (Professor J.Y. Simpson)

Wha kens on whatna Bethlehems
Earth twinkles like a star the nicht,
An' whatna shepherds lift their heids
In its unearthly licht?

'Yont a' the stars oor een can see
An' farther than their licht can fly,
'T mony an unco warl' the nicht
The fatefu' bairnies cry.

'T mony an unco warl' the nicht
The lift gaes black as pitch at noon,
An' sideways on their chests the heids
O' endless Christs roll doon.

An' when the earth's as cauld's the mune
An' a' its folk are lang syne deid,
On countless stars the babe maun cry
An' the Crucified maun bleed.

Hugh MacDiarmid (1892–1978)

Yont: beyond
Unco: strange
Lift (v.3): sky

Deathbed

Now, when the frail and fine-spun
Web of mortality
Gapes, and lets slip
What we have loved so long
From out our lighted present
Into the trackless dark.

We turn, blinded,
Not to the Christ in Glory,
Stars about his feet,

But to the Son of Man,
Back from the tomb,
Who built fires, ate fish,
Spoke with friends, and walked
A dusty road at evening.

Here, in this room, in
This stark and timeless moment,
We hear those footsteps

And
With suddenly lifted hearts
Acknowledge
The irrelevance of death.

Evangeline Paterson (20th century)

Passion Flower

And the flower weeps
        unbruised,
Lacrimae Christi,

For him who was silenced;

        whose advent
dumb bells in the dim light celebrate
        with wine song:

Messiah will come again,
After the argument in heaven;
Messiah will come again,
Lumen mundi...

Fingers of penitence
bring
to a palm grove
vegetable offering
with five
fingers of chalk.

Christopher Okigbo (1932–)

Parousia

I could imagine a biblical presence:
a darkening of matter like this charged
sky, before the coming of the storm,
the lime trees around the station
streaming with rain,
a stiffening, a scab of pus and blood,
a wound on the air, a voice above the rooves,

– but I think, if it came, there would be
something more subtle:
a blur at the corner of vision, a trick of the light,
or the notion that things have shifted

closer: streetlamps and walls,
privet hedges, trees, the neighbour's door,
intimate, all of a sudden, and out in the dark

the animals defined and understood
– vixen and weasel, barn own and pipistrelle –
granted their privileged moments to sleep and kill.

Companion self: not me, but echoes
breeding on the skin;
a half-life of touches and blows, the sub-microscopic
pattern of resurrection.
                                        I knew I could squat
in the fen-smell under the hedge
or walk away through fields and timber yards
to moorhens' nests and oildrums full of rain,

but somewhere along the way
I would meet the Christ:
a tripwire; a mat of hair; an open wound;
the silver of fish blood and bone
in the whites of his eyes.

There were borders I never crossed:
pools of goldenrod behind the barn,
harrows and tangles of wire
immersed in weed,

the meadow beyond our road, the purple woods,
the watergall, the sub-infinity
of oatfields at dawn

– but I knew he was always present, walking away
in the warmth of the ripening grain,
dangerous, graceful, bright as a circus cat,
or the man from the high wire, come down to touch the earth,

tasting the air, how it sweetens and turns to blood
in the throat, in the new-won flesh, in the sudden body.

It was less of a stream than a border:
a rill over wheat-coloured stones, then a sudden
dimming.
            And that was the place to cross,
treading the cold, my bare feet snagging a depth
of fish-skin and weed,
that was the kingdom of pike, where the body was laid
a finger's-depth under the sand.

The far side was stranger's country, a half-mile away:
a back road far in the heat, a gust of wind,
cow parsley, mare's tails, a glimmer of slate in the distance,
and out in the open field, a dog-fox
pausing in its stride, to scent the air,
the only spirit I could understand
the black awareness rooted in its eyes.

A heresy, but soul becomes
conceivable, immersed in viscera,
and mind endures, in wisps of meat and bone;
at twilight, crossing the river, I always knew
something was close, but all I ever saw
was blood-warm, vivid, wholly physical:
the sparrow-hawk sweeping the air, the questing owl,
the stoat in the wall, that knows where its hunger is going.

All resurrections are local:
footprints bleeding away
through marsh-grass and water,
a sound you can almost hear
of the flesh renewed
in the plashing of rain
or a quick trout
breaking the stream.

For the sign I have waited to see
is happening now
and always, in this white continuum
of frost and spawn:
the blood in a tangle of thorns
where it stiffens and pales,
the hard bud splitting through ice
and the nailed palm healing.

John Burnside (1955–)

Index of Authors

Index of First Lines

Acknowledgments

We would like to thank all those who have given us permission to include quotations in this book, as indicated in the list below. Every effort has been made to trace and acknowledge copyright holders of all the quotations included in this book. We apologize for any errors or omissions that may remain, and would ask those concerned to contact the publishers, who will ensure that full acknowledgment is made in the future.

Anonymous: 'The Dream of the Rood' from *The Anglo-Saxon World*, ed. Kevin Crossley-Holland, published by Oxford University Press.

Auden, W.H.: 'At the Manger Mary Sings' from *For the Time Being, Collected Poems by W.H. Auden*, published by Faber and Faber Ltd.

Awoonor, Kofi: 'Easter Dawn', published by Mbari Publications, Ibadan, Nigeria, 1964.

Berrigan, Daniel: 'Lazarus', published by The World Publishing Co.

Betjeman, John: 'Christmas' from *Collected Poems*, published by John Murray Publishers Ltd. Reprinted by permission.

Bridges, Robert: Extract from 'The Testament of Beauty' from *Poetical Works of Robert Bridges* (1936). Reprinted by permission of Oxford University Press.

Burnside, John: 'Simon of Cyrene' from *A Normal Skin*, copyright © 1997 John Burnside, and 'Parousia' from *Swimming in the Flood*, copyright © 1995 John Burnside, published by Jonathan Cape.

Campbell, Roy: 'To the Sun' from *Collected Works*, copyright © Francisco Campbell Custodio and Ad Donker Publishers. Reproduced by permission of Jonathan Ball Publishers Ltd.

Causley, Charles: 'Mother and Child', 'The Sheep on Blackening Hills', 'Ballad of the Bread Man', 'Emblems of the Passion' and 'I am the Great Sun' from *Collected Poems 1951–2000* by Charles Causley, published by Macmillan. Reproduced by permission of David Higham Associates Ltd.

Chesterton, G.K.: 'The House of Christmas' and 'The Donkey', reproduced by permission of A.P. Watt Ltd, on behalf of the Royal Literary Fund.

Cullen, Countee: Excerpt from 'Heritage' and 'Simon the Cyrenian Speaks', published in *Color*, copyright © 1925 Harper & Bros, New York. Renewed 1952 Ida M. Cullen. Copyrights administered by Thompson and Thompson, New York.

Fanthorpe, U.A.: 'This was the Moment', and 'Getting it Across', copyright © U.A. Fanthorpe, from *Standing To* (1982) reproduced by permission of Peterloo Poets.

Gould, Gerald: 'The Happy Tree', published by Victor Gollancz. Reproduced by permission of the Estate of Michael Ayrton.

Graves, Robert: 'In the Wilderness' from Complete Poems, published by

Carcanet Press Ltd, 1999. Reprinted by permission.

Heaney, Seamus: 'Cana Revisited' from *Door into the Dark*, published by Faber and Faber Ltd.

Hughes, Ted: 'Crow Blacker than Ever' from *Crow: From the Life and Songs of the Crow* and 'Being Christlike', from *New Selected Poems 1957–1994*, published by Faber and Faber Ltd. 'On the Death of Princess Diana', copyright © Ted Hughes.

Image, Selwyn: 'A Meditation for Christmas' from *The Oxford Book of English Verse*, published by Oxford University Press.

Jamie, Kathleen: 'Outreach' from *The Queen of Sheba*, published by Bloodaxe Books, 1994.

Kavanagh, Patrick: 'Street Corner Christ'. Reprinted by kind permission of the Trustees of the Estate of Patrick Kavanagh, c/o Peter Fallon, Literary Agent, Loughcrew, Oldcastle, Co. Meath, Ireland.

Kirkup, James: 'Cena', and Kenkyusha Publishing Co., Tokyo, where 'Cena' first appeared in his collection *Japan Physical* (1969), reprinted in *Selected Shorter Poems Vol. 2, Once and for All* Salzburg University Press (1996).

Knight, John: 'Father to the Man' from *Let there be God*, ed. T.H. Parker and F.J. Teskey.

Langland, William: 'Piers Plowman: The Harrowing of Hell', trs. Ronald Tamplin, copyright © Ronald Tamplin.

Lee, Laurie: 'Twelfth Night', published by Penguin. Reprinted by permission of the Peters, Fraser & Dunlop Group Ltd.

Lewis, C. Day: 'Pietà', written on the assassination of President John F. Kennedy, and 'In the Beginning was the Word' from *The Complete Poems*, published by Sinclair Stevenson (1992), copyright © 1992 in this edition The Estate of C. Day Lewis.

MacDiarmid, Hugh: 'The Innumerable Christ', from *Complete Poems*, published by Carcanet Press Ltd, 1993. Reprinted by permission.

Mason, R.A.K.: 'Footnote to John ii.4' and 'Judas Iscariot' from *The Penguin Book of New Zealand Verse*. Reproduced by permission of the Hocken Library, University of Otago.

Monro, Harold: 'Children of Love' from *Collected Poems of Harold Monro*. Reproduced by permission of Gerald Duckworth and Co. Ltd.

Morris, Mervyn: 'Joseph of Arimathaea' and 'Pilate' from *The Heinemann Book of Caribbean Poetry*.

Mtshali, Oswald: 'Ride upon the Death Chariot' from *Sounds of a Cowhide Drum*, published by Renoster Books, Cape Town, 1971.

Murray, Les: 'Animal Nativity', from *Collected Poems*, published by Carcanet Press Ltd, 1998. Reprinted by permission.

Okigbo, Christopher: 'Passion Flower' from *Heavensgate* Mbari Publications, Ibadan, Nigeria, 1961.

Paterson, Evangeline: 'Deathbed'. Reproduced by permission of the author.

Pilling, Christopher: From 'The Adoration of the Magi' from *The Oxford Book of Christmas Poems*, published by Oxford University Press.

Porter, Peter: 'The Unlucky Christ' from *Collected Poems* (1983). Reprinted by permission of Oxford University Press.

Pound, Ezra: 'Ballad of the Goodly Fere' from *Collected Shorter Poems*, published by Faber and Faber Ltd.

Prince, F.T.: 'Soldiers Bathing' from *Collected Poems* by F.T. Prince, published by Carcanet Press Ltd, 1993. Reprinted by permission.

Rock, Madeleine Caron: 'He is the Lonely Greatness' from *Poems of Today* and *Come Hither*, comp. Walter de la Mare, 3rd edition, 1957, copyright © 1927 Sidgwick and Jackson.

St John, Patricia: 'The Alchemist', published by Scripture Union.

Sandburg, Carl: 'Star Silver' from *The Sandburg Range*, copyright © 1957 Carl Sandburg and renewed 1985 by Margaret Sandburg, Janet Sandburg and Helga Sandburg Crile. Reprinted by permission of Harcourt Brace and Company.

Sandburg, Carl: 'Child' from *Chicago Poems*, copyright © 1916 Holt, Rinehart and Winston and renewed 1944 by Carl Sandburg. Reprinted by permission of Harcourt, Inc.

Sansom, Clive: 'Mary of Magdala' and 'Judas' from *The Witnesses*, published by Methuen. Reprinted by permission of David Higham Associates Ltd.

Shillito, Edward: 'He Showed them His Hands and His Side' from *Jesus of the Scars and Other Poems* copyright © 1927 Sidgwick and Jackson.

Sitwell, Edith: 'Still Falls the Rain' from *Collected Poems*, published by Sinclair Stevenson. Reproduced by permission of David Higham Associates Ltd.

Smith, Stevie: 'The Airy Christ', copyright © James MacGibbon.

Stevenson. Reproduced by permission of David Higham Associates Ltd.

Thomas, Dylan: 'This Bread I Break', published by J.M. Dent. Reprinted by permission of David Higham Associates Ltd.

Thomas, R.S.: 'Amen', 'Suddenly', 'Mediations', 'The Interrogation' and 'The Problem' from *Laboratories of the Spirit*, copyright © Gwydion Thomas. 'The Hand', 'In Church' and 'In a Country Church', from *Selected Poems 1946–1968*, published by Bloodaxe Books, 1986.

Underhill, Evelyn: 'Immanence', published by Addison Wesley Longman.

Updike, John: 'Seven Stanzas at Easter', from *Telephone Poles and Other Poems* by John Updike. Reproduced by permission of Penguin UK.

Virtue, Vivian: 'Waifs' from *The Penguin Book of Caribbean Verse* by Paula Burnett.

Walcott, Derek: *Midsummer* no. LIV and 'Easter' from *Collected Poems 1948–84*, published by Faber and Faber Ltd, 1984.

Yeats, W.B.: 'The Magi' and 'The Second Coming', reproduced by permission of A.P. Watt Ltd on behalf of Michael B. Yeats.